THE PEACEMAKER
AND ITS RIVALS

Peacemaker No. 1

Courtesy of John S. du Mont

The PEACEMAKER AND ITS RIVALS

An Account of the Single Action Colt

John E. Parsons

Skyhorse Publishing

Skyhorse Publishing books may be purchased in bulk at special discounts
for sales promotion, corporate gifts, fund-raising, or educational purposes.
Special editions can also be created to specifications. For details,
contact the Special Sales Department, Skyhorse Publishing, 307 West 36th
Street, 11th Floor, New York, NY 10018 or info@skyhorsepublishing.com.

Skyhorse® and Skyhorse Publishing® are registered trademarks of
Skyhorse Publishing, Inc.®, a Delaware corporation.

www.skyhorsepublishing.com

10 9 8 7 6 5 4 3 2 1

Library of Congress Cataloging-in-Publication Data is available on file.

ISBN: 978-1-62636-570-4

Printed in the United States of America

CONTENTS

FOREWORD   vii

I.   ANTECEDENT REVOLVERS   3

II.   EVOLUTION OF THE PEACEMAKER   17

III.   THE SCHOFIELD SMITH & WESSON   28

IV.   THE REMINGTON MODEL OF 1875   36

V.   CONTEMPORARY OPINIONS   46

VI.   MULTIBALL CARTRIDGES   56

VII.   OTHER RIVALS   64

VIII.   ADOPTION OF THE DOUBLE ACTION   73

IX.   POPULARITY OF THE MODEL "P"   84

X.   VARIATIONS AND TARGET TYPES   100

XI.   SERIAL NUMBERS AND SALES   111

XII.   VOLUME OF PRODUCTION BY CALIBRES   121

v

XIII.   PATENTS AND PIRATES   128

XIV.   SIGNIFICANCE OF THE REVOLVER   136

       APPENDIX: THE THUER CONVERSION   141

       NOTES   159

       BIBLIOGRAPHY   173

       INDEX   178

FOREWORD

IN introducing the subject of this study, I can do no better than to quote the words of Walter Prescott Webb, Professor of History at the University of Texas: [1]

The revolver as a factor in the development of America has never received serious consideration, either from the historian or the literary man. The former has neglected it entirely, while the latter has neither understood it nor its true place in our national life. Too frequently he has used it as his chief stock in trade in portraying certain striking types of American men—the Texas Ranger, the cowboy, or the bad man on horseback. The sensational story-writers, the moving pictures, and even worthier literary men, are loath to abandon this original idea.

These words were written in 1927, since which time the topic has received more adequate attention, though mainly from collectors and shooters of arms. Books written primarily by or for them have thoroughly catalogued the various kinds of American pistols and revolvers, including the Colt, but the significance of these weapons in the context of their times remains an inviting study. Make by make and model by model, this analysis is going forward as new sources of information are discovered or become available.

It is the purpose of this book to detail the life story of only one model of revolver, the single action Colt. Rivals and ramifications extending over a century are involved in the telling. For a collector there is ever the temptation to write in catalog form, and I cannot claim to have avoided it altogether. Even an historian or professional writer might find the material too factual for literary treatment. My own endeavor has been where possible to relate each arm described to its setting, and in this way to bring out its import in history.

In this enterprise I have incurred many obligations. Assistance of an essential nature is gratefully acknowledged from Robert E. Courtney, manager of the service department—arms division—of Colt's Manufacturing Company and a senior employee, to Charles H. Coles, curator of the Ulrich Museum and most senior in service at Colt's, to Thomas C. McPartland, advertising manager, and to Harry W. Lidstone in charge of sales. Without the courtesy and co-operation of those at Colt's in making available voluminous manufacturing records, this book could not have been carried to completion. Other source material was found at The New York Public Library, The New-York Historical Society in the Bella C. Landauer Business and Professional Collection, The Confederate Museum, Richmond, and The National Archives through its War Records Division. Names of collectors and institutions who have kindly supplied illustrations are noted in the captions, but I am particularly indebted for help and suggestions to Edwin Pugsley, Roy C. Horton, John Hintlian, James E. Serven, Wm. M. Locke, Stephen V. Grancsay, John S. du Mont, Gerald Fox, Charles W. Ferguson, Thomas E. Hall and S. Basil Haw. Last but not least I am grateful for the patient aid of Mary V. Farrell in preparing the manuscript for the printer.

J. E. P.

ADDENDA

SINCE original publication of this study, the reception of which by both collectors and shooters has been very heartening, further material quite unique in character has come to light. To present it graphically necessitates the insertion of fifteen additional plates. Their appearance immediately following this note is designed simply to avoid a repaging of text and index. While new readers may look upon these illustrations as an appendix, our hope is that old friends will find them a refresher.

The original contract of July 23, 1873, between Colt's and the Chief of Ordnance was discovered in an attic storeroom; it is reproduced through the courtesy of Colt's Manufacturing Company. Two previously unknown foreign trade sheets come from the files of James Joseph Goodbody, for many years an employee and the last manager of Colt's London Agency. Owners whose names appear in the captions have generously permitted unusual specimens to be illustrated; to them and to the Winchester Repeating Arms Company, for taking photographs, the author makes grateful acknowledgment.

J. E. P.

This Contract, made and entered into this *Twenty-third* day of *July* one thousand eight hundred and sixty- *seventy-three* between *the Colts Patent Firearms Manufacturing Company* of *Hartford, Conn.,* by *General M.B. Franklin, Vice President and General Agent of said Company* of ———— in the State of ———— Chief of Ordnance, acting of the first part, and the United States, by *Brig. Gen. A.B. Dyer,* under direction and by authority of the Secretary of War, for and in their behalf, of the second part, *WITNESSETH:* That the party of the first part does hereby contract and engage with the said United States to furnish

8000 Colts Army Revolvers, caliber forty-five hundredths of an inch (.45) on the following terms and conditions These revolvers are to be furnished each with a screw driver, and air, with said screw driver, the three same model as the pattern heretofore submitted to the Chief of Ordnance by said Colts Patent Firearms Manufacturing Company, the principal dimensions, however, being as follows:

Barrel, Length 7.48"; Diameter of bore 443" Number of grooves 6; Depth of grooves .01"
Chamber 16 .. ; Length .6225;
Cylinder, Length 1.608"; Number of chambers 6; Diameter .165"; Diameter of chamber { *.485" .482" .450"* }

It being agreed that minor modifications may be made by the Chief of Ordnance, should it be deemed by them advisable to do so, without in anywise altering the general design of the arm.

The Original Contract between the Chief of Ordnance and Colt's.
(Start of page 1.)

The revolver and appendages to be subject to inspection by United States inspectors in the same manner that United States arms are inspected, and cannot be received or paid for but as a fair inspection and are approved by the inspector;

Inspection to be delivered at the armory of the said Colt's Patent Fire Arms Manufacturing Company at Hartford, Conn., at the following rate, viz:

Deliveries to begin and continue, after six (6) weeks from the date of this contract, at the rate of fifty (50) per day, and when first thousand (700) are delivered, the rate to be increased to one hundred (100) per day until the whole number of eight thousand (8000) are delivered; and the party of the first part will have the right to deliver more rapidly, according to the number of arms before specified, if they can do so.

ALL THESE *Colt* Revolvers and appendages are to be delivered by the said party of the first part; and all claims under this contract, if transferred to another party, are to be by such transfer forfeited, saving the rights of the United States. Payments, in such funds as the Treasury Department may provide, for each delivery, are to be made on certificates of inspection and receipt by the United States Inspectors, at the rate of *thirteen* dollars (**$13**) for each revolver with its accompanying screw driver;

ALL THESE *Arms and appendages* are to be packed by the party of the first part in good and sufficient boxes of an approved pattern, *with fifty revolvers and appendages in each box, and the boxes properly labeled as to contents* for which a fair price, to be determined by the United States Inspector, will be allowed.

End of page 1 of the Original Contract

And the said part y of the first part do *es* further engage and contract, that no member of Congress, officer of the Army, or any agent of the military service, or other person forbidden by law so to do, *is, or shall be,* admitted to any share or part of this contract or agreement, or to any benefit to arise thereupon.

And it is hereby expressly provided, and this contract is upon the express condition, that if any such member of Congress, officer of the Army, or other person above named, *is, or shall be,* admitted to any share or part of this contract, or to any benefit to arise under it, or in case the part y of the first part shall in any respect fail to perform this contract on *its* part, the same may be, at the option of the United States, declared null and void, without affecting their right to recover for defaults which may have occurred.

It is further stipulated and agreed, that if any default shall be made by the part y of the first part in delivering all or any of the articles mentioned in this contract, of the quality and at the times and place therein provided, that then, in that case, the said part will forfeit and pay to the United States the sum of *money not exceeding fifteen thousand* —————— dollars, as agreed, and liquidated damages.

The said *Colts Patent Firearms Manufacturing Company* shall indemnify the United States and all persons acting under them for all liability on account of any patent rights heretofore granted by the United States; and in case of overwhelming and unforeseen accident by fire or otherwise, the circumstances shall be taken into equitable consideration by the United States before claiming forfeiture for non-delivery at the times specified.

Beginning of page 2 of the Original Contract

And the said UNITED STATES do hereby contract and engage with the said part _y_ of the first part as follows: That for each of the articles herein contracted for which shall be delivered, inspected, and approved as aforesaid, there shall be paid, in the funds aforesaid, to the said Colts Patent Firearms Manufacturing Company, or their attorney,

the so remanufac , heirs, executors, or administrators, on bills in triplicate, made in approved form, and duly authenticated by the proper officers of the Ordnance Department, the sum of thirteen dollars ($ 18) for each revolver with its appendages complete, and for each packing to a fair price to be determined as above stated

Signed, sealed, and delivered

in presence of—

Geo R Ellis
Capt of Ord.

APPROVED:

A B Dyer

W B Franklin
Brevet Lieut Colpt Cottituullo

A B Dyer

Brig. General,
Chief of Ordnance.

SEAL.

SEAL.

SEAL.

[40-cent Revenue Stamp here.]

Continuation of page 2 of the Original Contract

Know all men by these Presents, That we, Colt's Patent Firearms Manufacturing Company, by H. B. Franklin, Vice President and Genl. agent, in the State of Connecticut, of Hartford, in the State of Connecticut, as principal, and Roswell A. Harris, and Horace Lord , of Hartford, as sureties, are held and firmly bound unto the United States of America in the penal sum of fifteen thousand dollars, to be paid to the said United States, or to their certain attorney; for which payment, well and truly to be made, we bind ourselves, our heirs, executors, and administrators, jointly and severally, firmly by these presents. Sealed with our seals, and dated the 23 rd day of July A. D. 1873.

Whereas the above-bounden Colt's Patent Firearms Manufacturing Company has entered into the contract with the United States set forth in the foregoing covenant: Now, therefore, the conditions of this obligation are such that if the said Colt's Patent Firearms Manufacturing Company heirs, executors, or administrators, shall well and faithfully fulfill each and every one of the aforesaid covenants, this obligation to be null and void; otherwise, to be and remain in full force and virtue.

W. B. Franklin
G. Fred. Leigh Col. Ord. Mville

R. A. Harris   [SEAL.]

Horace Lord   [SEAL.]

                                [SEAL.]

End of page 2 of the Original Contract

General Custer and his Indian Scouts, 1874

Courtesy of Custer Battlefield National Monument

[FORM No. 39.]

Certificate No. 2, on order of July 25, 1873.

I hereby Certify, That I have inspected and approved

One thousand Colts Army Revolvers, 45/in. Caliber
One thousand Screw Drivers
Twenty Packing Boxes

Also Spare Parts as per Invoice sent on the 12th inst., as per
Specifications on next Pages.

furnished by Colts Pat. Fire Arms Mfg. Co., of Hartford, Conn. under the order of, or contract with the United States dated July 23rd, 1873 : And I further Certify, That the said Arms & Appendages have been inspected according to the Regulations established by the ORDNANCE DEPARTMENT for the proof and inspection of Small Arms before their reception for the SERVICE OF THE UNITED STATES; that they conform to the standard models and established gauges; that they are of good quality and workmanship; that they are securely packed in good, strong boxes, and that they are in all respects conformable to said order or contract. I also Certify, That, according to my best judgment, the value of each packing-box is Five dollars cents.

GIVEN under my hand at Hartford, Conn., this 12 day of December, 1873.

APPROVED:

Jno R. Edie
Capt of Ord.
Inspector.

O. W. Ainsworth
Assistant Inspector.

Received, at Springfield, Mass this 15 day of Dec. 1873 the Ordnance and Ordnance Stores enumerated in the foregoing Recapitulation.

Edward Ingersoll
PM & O S K.
Maj USA

[TRIPLICATE.]

Inspection Certificate No. 2, dated December 12, 1873

The United States Ordnance Department, **DR.**

To The Colts Patent Fire Arms Mfg Co , of Hartford Coun

DATE.		DOLLARS.	CTS.
Dec . 12. 1873.	1000 Colts Army Revolvers, 45 Caliber		
	Appendages , @ 13°°	13,000	00
	20 Packing Boxes " 5°°	100	00
	Spare Parts as per Invoices		
	100 Hammers @ .65 65.00		
	100 Searsprings " .02 2.00		
	100 Hands " .12 12.00		
	100 " Springs " .02 2.00	102	00
	100 Latch " " .01 1.00		
	100 Triggers " .10 10.00		
	100 Mainsprings " .10 10.00		
	TOTAL............................$	13,202	00

The above account, amounting to *Thirteen thousand two hundred two* — — — *⁰⁰⁄₁₀₀ dollars, is correct.*

_____ Capt of Ord. Inspector.

I request that the amount of the above account may be paid to the order of *Colts Patent Fire Arms Mfg Co* at Hartford Conn.

W B Franklin
Vice Prest Secdly

NOTE.—This request will be signed by the claimant, after inserting the *name* and *post office address* of the party to whom the Treasury draft is to be remitted.

(B. 27. 3. 63. 10. M.)

[Inspection Certificate No. 1 was dated Nov. 26, 1873. It is not reproduced because Colt's copy was unsigned. Certificate No. 3 was dated Jan. 1, No. 4, Jan. 15, No. 5, Jan. 29, No. 6, Feb. 13, No. 7, Feb. 28, and No. 8, March 14, 1874. Each covered 1,000 pistols.]

RECAPITULATION.

DATE WHEN EACH LOT WAS RECEIVED.	QUANTITY RECEIVED.	ARTICLES RECEIVED
December 12-18>8	1000	Colt's Army Revolvers, 45 Cal.
	1000	Screw Drivers
	20	Packing Boxes
	100	Hammers
	100	Sear springs
	100	Bolts
	100	" Spring
	100	Latch "
	100	Trigger
	100	Mainsprings
TOTAL............		

Recapitulation on Inspection Certificate No. 2

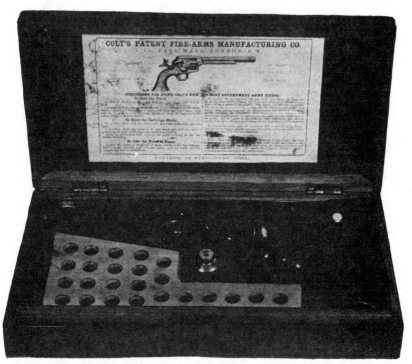

London Cased .450 Boxer, marked "DEPOT 14 PALL MALL LONDON"

COLT'S
American Government Cavalry Revolver,
·450 Cal.

Known as " **FRONTIER PISTOL,** *" if made for the .440 cal.*
Cartridge, as used in the <u>Colt and Winchester Magazine Rifle</u>.

Extract from SIR SAMUEL BAKER'S " Wild Beasts and their Ways," Page 217.

"Early on the following morning I sent for the bear's skin. It proved to be a large silver-tipped, and a close examination exhibited the difficulties of the encounter during darkness. . . . . The 'eight's' was the only bullet that struck the bear! This had entered between the shoulders vertically. . . . The bullet had passed through the centre of the heart, and had escaped near the brisket, having penetrated completely through this formidable animal. Upon my return to England I immediately purchased a similar Revolver of Messrs. Colt & Co.— the long ' Frontier' Pistol, 450 bullet."

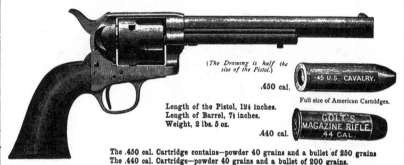

(The Drawing is half the size of the Pistol.)

.450 cal.

Full size of American Cartridges.

Length of the Pistol, 12¼ inches.
Length of Barrel, 7½ inches.
Weight, 2 lbs. 5 oz.

.440 cal.

The .450 cal. Cartridge contains—powder 40 grains and a bullet of 250 grains.
The .440 cal. Cartridge—powder 40 grains and a bullet of 200 grains.

Price £5. Plated £5 10s. Case complete, to order, £1 5s. Holster Belt and Pouch, £1.

American Cartridges, .45 cal. 10s. per 100. | English Cartridges, .455 cal. 9s. per 100.
     „   „   .44 cal. 10s.   „ | „   „   .450 cal. 8s.   „

Complete Set of Reloading Tools for .45 and .44 cal. Cartridges, Bullet Mould included,
22s. per set.

Primers, per 1000, 7s.   Capped Shells, per 1000, 50s.   Bullets, per 1000, 25s.

This Pistol, for fully twenty years now, has kept up its reputation for being superior to all others in disabling powers, accuracy of fire, and, before all, in durability. During the three meetings of the National Rifle Association at Wimbledon and Bisley Common, in 1889, 1890, and 1891, the only years of which the Company has full records, these Pistols were the preferred weapons, and they won most of the Prizes, while more than sixty thousand shots were fired with them without a **SINGLE** *mishap occurring. The United States Cavalry use no other.*

London Price List, 1895

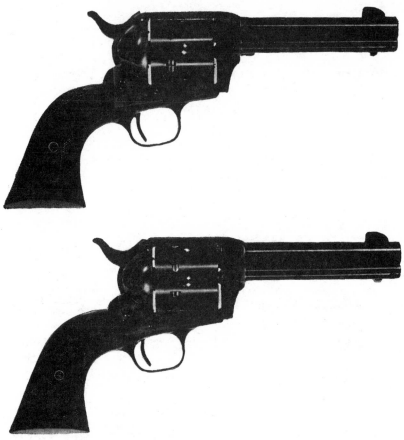

Magnums for the Battle of Britain

Broad Arrow Stamp

One of General Patton's Revolvers
Courtesy of West Point Museum

Oklahoma Marshal's Gold Plated .45
Courtesy of Herb Glass

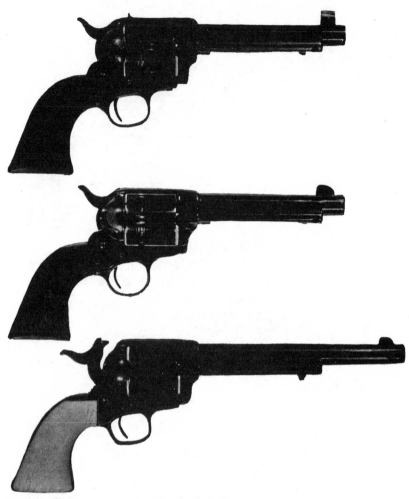

Special Target Model, 1888, marked "DEPOT 14 PALL MALL LONDON"
Peacemaker with D.A. Cylinder
Single Action in .44 R.F.

THE PEACEMAKER
AND ITS RIVALS

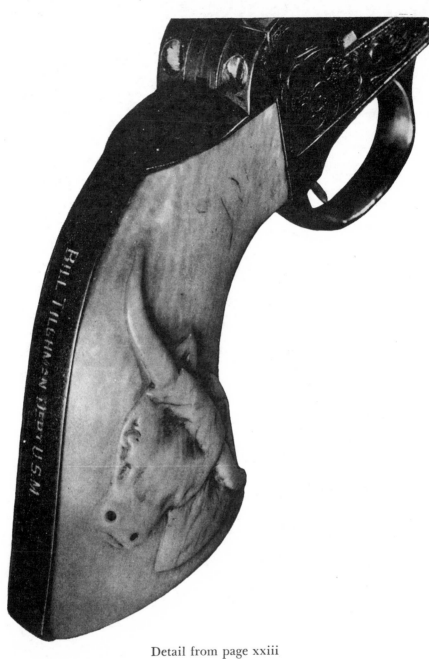

Detail from page xxiii

Courtesy of Herb Glass

I

ANTECEDENT REVOLVERS

IN WRITING of the single action Colt whose original trade name was the Peacemaker, care must be taken in the use of the word "first." Just as the Colt was not the first revolver invented, neither was the Peacemaker the original metallic cartridge revolver of military calibre, nor even the initial weapon of this kind of Colt manufacture. Yet it was and is a "first" in many ways. It was the first cartridge revolver to be officially adopted by the United States Army. Thereafter it prevailed over all rivals in trials conducted by the Ordnance Department, until the single action system was superseded. By all odds, it was the favorite choice among hand firearms of frontiersmen and cowboys. It has enjoyed the longest popularity of any model of revolver yet made and it remains the outstanding leader among weapons of its kind in numbers produced. But the story of the Peacemaker is more than a series of statistical superlatives, for a life span from the Cheyenne War to the Battle of Britain necessarily encompasses a lot of history. In the making of this history the single action Colt has become as much a part of American folklore as the picturesque users of the gun itself.

For the progenitors of the Peacemaker one must go back to the cap-and-ball "Paterson," the earliest revolver invented by Samuel Colt and dated by his first American patent of February 25, 1836. Features of this arm, which derives its

3

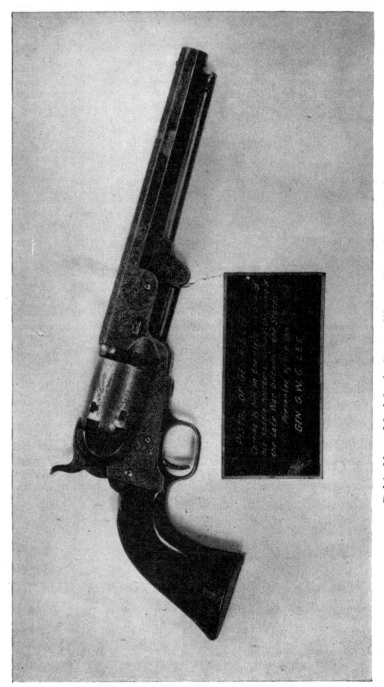

Colt's Navy Model of 1851, calibre .36, made c. 1855

Courtesy of The Confederate Museum

name from having been made at Paterson, New Jersey, by the Patent Arms Manufacturing Company, are traceable in all later revolvers of Colt design, even down to the present day. Yet it was the next model, made after a lapse of years at Whitneyville, Connecticut, with modifications worked out by Colt and Captain Samuel H. Walker, that gave the succeeding line of pistols to and including the subject of this study their more precise form, and great utility. This weapon of 1847, known as the "Walker," while of considerably greater dimensions than later models, achieved a minimum and simplicity of working parts never bettered in percussion revolver design. From it derived in sequence, the 1848 "Dragoon," the 1851 "Navy" and the military models developed just before the War Between the States, the latter being the immediate cap-and-ball ancestors of the Peacemaker.

In the War of 1861-1865 the hand firearm used more than any other on both sides was the .44 calibre percussion Colt revolver, Army Model of 1860. For the Union Army this statement is susceptible of statistical proof, since a Congressional investigation of the purchase of arms during the War has provided very complete figures on procurements by the Ordnance Department.[1] Of nearly 400,000 Colt revolvers manufactured from 1861 to 1865, the Ordnance Department bought directly 129,156 of Army or .44 calibre and 2,056 of Navy or .36 calibre. These were obtained under a series of contracts with Colt's Patent Firearms Manufacturing Company dating from May 4, 1861, to November 10, 1863. In the early months of the War the Department also secured from some twenty dealers, of which Joseph C. Grubb & Co. of Philadelphia, B. Kittredge & Co. of Cincinnati, and Schuyler, Hartley & Graham of New York were the prin-

[1] Reference notes to all chapters are on pages 159-172.

Pair of Colt's Army Model of 1860, calibre .44, inscribed "Gen. John H. Morgan Kentucky"

cipal ones, lots of Colt revolvers amounting to about 12,000 Navy and 2,500 Army size, bringing the grand total of Ordnance Department procurements to some 146,000. A large number of pistols were also supplied to troops by the States or purchased by officers and men with their own funds. The number of Colts used in the War would undoubtedly have been greater still had not a disastrous fire at the Colt factory in February, 1864, destroyed the building where the revolvers were made.

The revolver next in popularity to the Colt was the Remington, of which 115,563 in .44 calibre and 12,251 in .36 calibre were procured directly, plus about 4,000 in both sizes from dealers. Army contracts with E. Remington & Sons ran from June 13, 1862, to October 24, 1864, the last delivery of revolvers being made in March of 1865. Not all of these were issued, since it is of record that the Ordnance Department subsequently sold off 10,000 of .44 calibre and exchanged 5,000 more Remington percussion revolvers for an equal number of single shot breechloading pistols of .50 calibre.[2] Twenty-five dollars a revolver was the first contract price for .44 Colts, but the cost dropped to $14.50 and then $14 in 1862 when competition from Remington and other makers developed.[3] Remingtons were first sold for $15 and later $12, but in the final contract of October 24, 1864, when there was apparently no competition from Colt's, the price rose to $15.50.

In the Confederate Army the preference for the Colt was more decided, although not as easily demonstrated. During the War arms of Northern make were not readily obtainable in the South. Importation of pistols from abroad and a limited manufacture of replicas at home were the only direct means of procurement. Yet one has only to view the assortment of pistols preserved in the Confederate Museum at

Richmond to realize that the genuine Colt revolver, and particularly the most up-to-date army model, was by far the favorite firearm of Southern officers and cavalrymen.[4] For every Adams, Le Mat or Remington in the collection, there are at least five Colts, of which some two-thirds are .44 calibre of the 1860 Model. Some of these belonged to regular officers prior to the beginning of the conflict, but many, judging from condition and serial numbers, were battlefield captures.[5] The Confederate soldier recognized clearly the most effective military pistol of the time, and took the shortest route to its possession.

After the War the large supply of Colt .44 percussion pistols continued in military service, as well as the model of Remington army revolver introduced in 1863, a solid frame type of like calibre. That these percussion arms remained the latest in use for several years is indicated by a letter of a correspondent signing himself "R. A." [Regular Army?] published in the *Army and Navy Journal* of March 16, 1867:[6]

Sir: It is passing strange that while so much is being done in the way of perfecting the rifle and carbine, we hear nothing of an improved Army pistol. There are as many different pocket pistols, revolvers and repeaters as there are breech-loading rifles, but most of them are poor affairs for troops, and Colt's and Remington's Army pistols are still the best we have for the service; but we greatly need a better weapon of this kind. We want a pistol to use the metallic cartridge, of the calibre to be adopted for

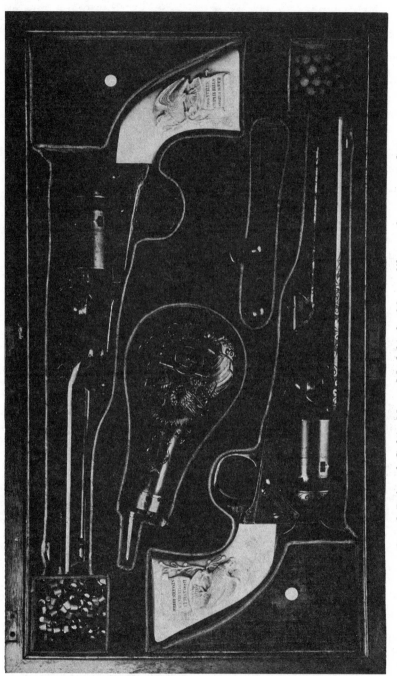

Cased Pair of Colt's Navy Model of 1861, calibre .36, presented to
Maj. Gen. Sheridan

Courtesy of The Smithsonian Institution

the new carbines (.45 or .50); or the Colt and Remington pistols might be altered to use metallic explosive cartridges, by cutting off the rear of the cylinder, so as to make it similar to Smith & Wesson's pistol cylinders; shortening the space in which the cylinder plays, and altering the hammer slightly. Everyone in the Army knows the great inconvenience of loading and capping an army pistol while in motion on horseback, and also the great number of pistol cartridges that are destroyed in the cartridge box, and in loading. With the metallic cartridge this waste does not occur. . . .

The Remington appears to have been the first revolver converted to cartridge loading to reach the hands of troops. A few specimens are known bearing on the altered cylinder the patent date "APRIL 3ᴰ, 1855," [7] thus raising the presumption that the alteration was licensed under the Rollin White patent for a bored-through cylinder. The debates in Congress on a bill which would have granted a rehearing of Rollin White's petition for extension of his patent indicate that he and Smith & Wesson had given the Government the right to use the patent and a release for past use. [8] But these licenses were not granted until late in 1869, and then only as a means of meeting the objections of the Ordnance Department to the extension. Where the converting was initially done is perhaps suggested by a listing in an early advertisement of the Union Metallic Cartridge Co. There the .46 calibre rimfire cartridge which the converted Remington utilized is described as "adapted to Remington's S. & W. Metallic cartridge Army revolver." [9]

Colt's meanwhile had not been idle in attempting to meet the requirements of the service. But the obstacle of the Rollin White patent precluded that company for several years from producing a breechloading revolver of military calibre that was both legitimate and practical. The story of

Remington Alteration, calibre .46, under Rollin White Patent

Courtesy of Winchester Repeating Arms Company

Colt's unsatisfactory experiment with the front loading Thuer alteration, which, though submitted to the ordnance authorities of both the United States and Great Britain, was purchased by neither government nor issued to troops, has been told in an article in *The American Rifleman* of April, 1949. This has been reprinted by the kind permission of that magazine in the Appendix.

From a Remington Price List c. 1872

Courtesy of G. Charter Harrison, Jr.

Conversion of the Remington soon led to criticism of the continued use by the military of the arm in its percussion form. Thus the *Army and Navy Journal,* in an editorial of September 25, 1869, commented: [10]

Officers of the Cavalry regiments stationed in the Indian country complain that many of the arms issued by the Government to their commands do not come up to the standard of efficiency which the peculiar nature of frontier service demands. . . . The Remington revolver, adopted as the standard arm of the service, also comes in for its share of censure, at least those belonging to the first and imperfect issue of several years ago. . . . The Remington revolver of *recent* issue is an undeniably good weapon. Its range is great and it can be relied on for accuracy. It is the old issue to which exceptions are taken.

Portions of the editorial not quoted confirm that the later and more satisfactory Remington was an improved model, *i.e.*, a conversion. The *Journal* dwelt at length on the inadequacy of muzzle-loading or single-shot arms in Indian war-

From a Remington Price List c. 1872

Courtesy of G. Charter Harrison, Jr.

fare, reaching the conclusion that Captain Fetterman's command could have held out until relieved if it had been armed with breechloading repeaters. This incident, which took place December 21, 1866, near Fort Phil Kearney in Wyoming, was a forerunner of Custer's last stand a decade later. Captain Fetterman, who had boasted that given eighty men he would "ride through the whole Sioux Nation," was sent out from the fort to relieve a wood train. Disregarding cautionary orders he chased a few mounted Indians into an ambush of several thousand Cheyennes and Sioux. His command of eighty men was split, surrounded and wiped out in about forty minutes. The Indians were armed almost entirely with bows and arrows, only six of the dead soldiers showing gunshot wounds. Some of the troops had Sharps carbines, others Springfield muzzle-loaders. Two frontiersmen in the party who also lost their lives were armed with Henry repeating rifles.[11]

After the Fetterman massacre the Indians, taking as it were a leaf from the book of the Confederates, made much use of captured Army firearms, including revolvers. An inventory of 410 arms taken from the Sioux and Cheyennes in 1877 included 123 revolvers, of which 69 were Colts and 41 Remingtons. Most of these were battered and unserviceable, at least by Army standards, although the ordnance officer examining them reported that "many of them could be used by so enterprising an enemy as the American Indian." These hand arms were with one exception cap-and-ball revolvers, which are known to have been used by the Indians in their fight with Custer on the Little Big Horn. There is also a record of several cartridge Colts, a pair of Smith & Wessons and a Schofield surrendered by the Cheyennes in 1878.[12] The utilization by the Indians of such arms affords perhaps another example that the keenest judge of the value of a military weapon is the enemy. Indian accounts of the capture of cartridge revolvers in the campaigns of 1876 are given in George Bird Grinnell's *The Fighting Cheyennes*. He records that the Indians habitually saved all metallic cartridge cases and with reloading outfits, powder and lead acquired by trade, were able to keep themselves supplied with ammunition for breechloading weapons.[13] This adaptability is noted in a contemporary report of an experienced Indian fighter, Major George B. Sanford, 1st Cavalry, as follows: [14]

Years of constant warfare have made of the Indians of our western territories partisan warriors, unequalled probably in their special mode of warfare by any people on earth. . . . The whole life of an Indian warrior from his boyhood is a constant preparation for the day of battle. Prompt to learn everything pertaining to warfare, they have copied from us, their hereditary enemies, whatever could be useful to them, while discarding such portions of our military system as would interfere with the personal liberty of the individual.

Comment on the lessons of the Fetterman massacre, the less disastrous Wagon Box fight of August 2, 1867, and Colonel Forsyth's successful stand at the Arikaree River in September, 1868,[15] undoubtedly prompted the appointment by the War Department of the Small Arms and Accoutrements Board which met at St. Louis early in 1870. Submitted for its examination were, besides a variety of long arms, several Remington .44 calibre revolvers, both percussion and altered to cartridge loading in four different styles; a Smith & Wesson .44 calibre revolver, precursor of the American Model; several National Arms and Whitney revolvers, and the Remington single shot pistol of .50 calibre, later known as the Army Model of 1871. No Colt example, altered or otherwise, was among the pistols submitted. The Board selected in the order of relative merit the Remington single shot, the Smith & Wesson, and one of the Remington revolver alterations. Its findings were reported in the *Army and Navy Journal* of July 23, 1870, as follows: [16]

The Remington is the only single-barrelled pistol submitted. It is an excellent weapon but should be so modified as to load at the half-cock.

The Smith & Wesson is decidedly superior to any other revolver submitted. It should be modified as follows, viz.: made centre fire; the cylinder lengthened so as to close the space in front of the breech-block, and counter sunk to cover the rim of the cartridge; calibre increased to the standard.

.   .   .   .

Pistols and revolvers should have the "saw-handle" so shaped that in bringing the weapon from the holster to an aim, it will not be necessary to change the first grasp or bend the wrist.

.   .   .   .

When time will permit, cavalry troops should be instructed in the use of all these arms; and all should be kept on hand with small bodies on the frontier, where every variety of cavalry service may be required.

The Board's first choice of pistol, the Remington single shot, seems singularly inappropriate for Indian warfare. That it was never intended for this purpose may be inferred from the comments in the report that "cavalry armed with the sabre should have one or two single-barrelled pistols as a substitute for the carbine" and that "cavalry armed with the carbine should have a revolver as a substitute for the sabre." In other words, where sabres were appropriate the Remington pistol would do instead of the single shot carbine. Imaginative illustrations to the contrary, the sabre was not usually carried in Indian campaigns.[17] The Chief of Ordnance, Brevet Major General A. B. Dyer, whose views were approved by General Sherman and the Secretary of War, recommended the purchase of "1,000 Remington single-barrelled pistols, calibre 50, and 1,000 Smith & Wesson revolvers of same calibre as our army revolvers" and the alteration of "1,000 Remington revolvers after the plan of #2, these pistols to be issued for comparative trial in service." While the details of the several Remington alterations are not given, it may be assumed that the model selected was that which the Remington Company subsequently advertised as the "Improved Army Model."

II

EVOLUTION
OF THE PEACEMAKER

TRANSITION of Army handarms from cap-
and-ball to metallic cartridge was officially fore-
cast in the Report of the Chief of Ordnance for 1871, as follows: [1]

A small number of revolvers (pistols) which use the primed
metallic cartridge, have been made and issued to troops, and the
few reports upon them which have been received at this Bureau
show that they are greatly superior to the revolvers which use
the paper cartridges, and must supersede them in the service. As
soon as a proper model can be selected it should be adopted.

Cartridge issues for the fiscal years ending June 30, 1872
and 1873, afford an indication of the pistols then in the hands
of troops. In the first year the Ordnance Department issued
to regular army units 317,114 paper pistol cartridges, calibre
.44; 5,000 of the same, calibre .36; 219,880 metallic centerfire pistol cartridges, calibre .44; and 130,088 cartridges for
the Smith & Wesson .44 (American Model). In the next year
paper cartridges continued to bulk large at 367,988 for .44
calibre but only 480 in .36. Three varieties of metallic cartridges in .44 calibre were issued: 40,700 "Colt's altered" [rim-
fire?], 19,200 "Colt's center-fire," and 21,130 Smith & Wesson.[2]
July, 1872-June, 1873, also was the period during which 1,529
Remington single shot pistols were issued, with 167,000
rounds of .50 calibre ammunition for them.

17

The categories of "Colt's altered" and "Colt's center-fire" reflect the development by Charles B. Richards of the alteration of the Colt .44 Army revolver patented in his name by the Colt Company on July 25, 1871. This was the forerunner of the open top .44 calibre Cartridge Model of 1872, soon supplanted by the .45 calibre Army Model of 1873, whose first commercial name was the Peacemaker. There is evidence that both preliminary Richards models were issued by the Army as well as the last. In the initial report on the Model of 1873 from the Springfield Armory under date of December 27, 1872,[3] Captain John R. Edie makes the statement that

The new model Colt's revolver is not an alteration of their old revolver for paper cartridges, as is the model now in service. It is made with a solid frame, inclosing the cylinder, and into which the barrel is screwed. The cylinder is of greater diameter, and a little shorter than the old one. The hand which rotates the cylinder is an improvement, having two fingers, one of which reinforces the other, giving a considerable gain of power. The ejector is similar to the old one, but one end of the ejector tube is set in the frame, the other being fastened to the barrel by a screw. The base pin is held by a screw through the frame.

This revolver is supplied with a safety notch, on which it can be carried without the firing pin touching the cartridge. The other parts are essentially the same as in the old model.

The distinctions pointed out by Captain Edie clearly identify what he calls "the model now in service" as the standard type of Richards conversion. The open top Model of 1872, which was a transition design rather than an alteration, is also described in a supplementary report of Captain Edie's under date of February 7, 1873, "on a new model of Colt's revolver, received from the Ordnance Office October 31, 1872":

To distinguish between this revolver and the one reported upon December 27, 1872, I will call the latter No. 1 and the former No. 2.

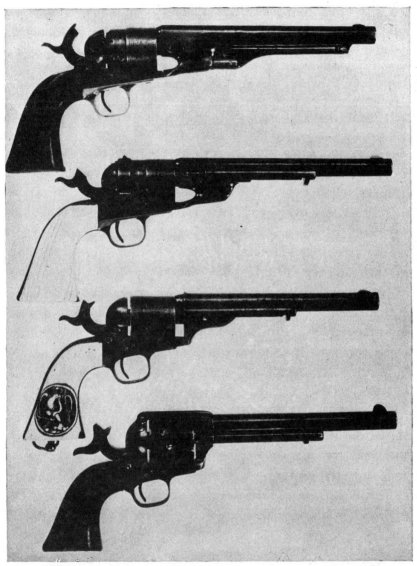

Colt's Army Model of 1860, Richards' Conversion, and Models of 1872 and 1873

Photograph courtesy of Winchester Repeating Arms Company

Colt's No. 2 is like No. 1 in the "lock," "hammer," "cylinder stop" and "revolving finger," but like the old model (now in service) in the general form of its frame and barrel. Its extreme length is about .5″ less than that of the old model, and it is 3.5 ounces lighter. It is also about 1.5 ounces lighter than No. 1 (new model). It has no firing pin, the cartridge being struck directly (the same as in No. 1) by the point of the hammer.

The object of Captain Edie's examinations was, as directed by the Chief of Ordnance, to test the two Colt's revolvers against a slightly modified version of the American Model of the Smith & Wesson, of which 1,000 had been purchased in 1870. For the purposes of the test all three pistols were chambered for service ammunition of .44 calibre. The particulars of the comparative trial of Colt's No. 1 and the Smith & Wesson, and the finding in favor of the former are given in an extract from Ordnance Notes, No. V, reproduced in Haven & Belden, *A History of the Colt Revolver*. They will only be summarized here. On firing each of the pistols 800 rounds or more, the better functioning of the Colt was evident throughout. The Smith & Wesson tended to clog, and was difficult to dismount for cleaning. The Colt was found to have fewer, simpler and stronger parts, not subject to as great stress as in the Smith & Wesson, whose only superiority noted was its speed of ejecting empty cartridges. In firing for accuracy the Colt had a mean absolute deviation at fifty yards of 3.11 inches as compared to 4.39 inches for the Smith & Wesson, and for penetration an average at twenty-five yards of 4.1 inches as compared to 3.35.

As between the two Colt models, Captain Edie reported that "the record for accuracy and penetration shows slightly better for the Colt's revolver No. 2 than for the No. 1, but the general working of the latter was the most satisfactory, and I think the construction of the revolver is better. The form of the 'frame' gives greater strength, and also gives more space for the cylinder, which, together with the improved 'base-pin' reduces the tendency to clog when fired. The No. 1 is more readily dismounted for cleaning than the No. 2." This report sounded the requiem for the open top Model of 1872, and serves to explain why that model is a comparative rarity today. Specimens take several forms regarding style of handle, straps, firing pin for rim or centerfire, and markings, with serial numbers ranging into the 5,300s.

It was not, however, until after two further trials of Smith & Wesson pistols that the initial finding in favor of the Colt was implemented by a Government order. First Captain Edie examined a Smith & Wesson Model of 1873, which differed from the earlier type in its ejecting mechanism. He also tested the first model of the Schofield Smith & Wesson designed by Major George W. Schofield, an officer of the Tenth Cavalry. The latter had taken out a patent dated June 29, 1871, on a barrel-latch mounted on the frame rather than on the barrel and designed to be closed by the hammer before firing. He also held a patent of April 22, 1873, on an ejector whose spring was housed inside its stem and on a rotating crank enclosed by the recoil plate. Captain Edie found that this revolver was an improvement over the American Model in its extractor and revolving apparatus, but that "the number of parts was reduced by *one only* in the whole revolver, still leaving it objectionable for troops, in comparison with a weapon of less number and more simple ones." The final result was indicated by an entry of June 26, 1873, in Ordnance Notes, No. V: "As the reports . . . plainly show the superiority of the Colt revolver (last model) over all others tried, the Chief of Ordnance has been authorized by the War Department to purchase 8,000 of these arms for the cavalry arm of the service."

These were chambered for .45 calibre, centerfire cartridges containing a 230 grain bullet and 28 grains of black powder, but they would also take Colt commercial cartridges of up to 40 grains. Correspondence in the Springfield Armory files indicates that while the order was being filled the specifica-

---

NATIONAL ARMORY.

Springfield, Mass.

— ◆•◆•◆

THIS BOX CONTAINS

50 Colt's Revolvers, Caliber .45,

5 Main Springs,	10 Back Strap Screws, Assorted,
5 Gate Springs,	5 Hammer Screws,
5 Hand Springs,	5 Trigger Screws,
5 Ejector Springs,	5 Stop Bolt Screws,
5 Sear and Stop Bolt Springs (combined),	5 Center Pin Screws,
5 Firing Pins,	5 Ejector Tube Screws,
5 Firing Pin Rivets,	5 Gate Catch Screws,
5 Guard Screws (long),	5 Main Spring Screws.
5 Guard Screws (short),	5 Sear and Stop Bolt Spr. Screws (combined),

50 Screw Drivers.

Courtesy of John Hintlian

tions were changed to provide for six grooves instead of seven in the rifling. This was to have one uniform turn in 16 inches rather than a progressive twist in 37.2. Sighting for 25 yards was also specified, as was a front sight of steel. The report of the Chief of Ordnance for 1873 states: [4]

The general and constant demand from the field for revolvers using metallic ammunition, together with the urgent necessity for some improved weapon to replace the revolvers previously used in service using the paper or linen cartridge, caused early efforts to be made to reach a solution of this very difficult problem. After trials in the field of two kinds, and experimental trials of improved models, this Bureau recommended for approval the purchase of a sufficient number of the Colts to supply the cavalry arm of the service. They are now being made, and it is hoped that the whole number will be in the hands of troops before the next spring.

Immediately following such adoption by the War Department, the identical arm was extensively advertised for sale to the public by B. Kittredge & Co. of Cincinnati, agents for the Colt Company, as the Peacemaker.[5] The great and lasting commercial success of the single action Colt in a variety of of calibres and models will be dealt with in a later chapter. Reports of the Ordnance Department give procurements of the Colt .45 and issues to Regular Army units in fiscal years as follows: [6]

	Procured	Issued
1874	8,000	6,801
1875	6,400	2,750
1876	670	949
1877	2,003	2,777
1878	—	658
1879	3,000	873
1880	2,000	1,185
1881	1,000	938
1882	1,000	840
1883	1,000	1,359
1884	2,002	765
1885	2,000	592
1886	2,000	735
1887	2,000	776
1888	—	1,132
1889	—	1,394
1890	1,000	2,575
1891	3,000	968
1892	—	1,023
1893	—	651
Total . . .	37,075	29,741

In each of these years beginning with 1875, there were additional issues made by the Ordnance Department to militia of the various states and territories amounting altogether to 10,107 pistols, and in certain years beginning with 1879 to departments of the Federal Government. As the amount of these issues, plus those to the Regular Army, exceeds by several thousand the total procured, it is apparent that some of the militia and departmental issues were of used or repaired arms which had been returned to Government arsenals from the Army.

At the time of Custer's fight on the Little Big Horn in June, 1876, over 10,000 single action Colts had been issued in the Army. Custer's regiment, the Seventh Cavalry, was armed with them, according to the recollections of Sergeant Charles A. Windolph, a member of Company H, which was part of Major Reno's column that survived the battle.[7] Another survivor testified soon afterwards that "there was not a sabre in the command. They had revolvers and carbines; revolvers loaded and two additional loadings, 18 rounds, 50 carbine cartridges in belt and 50 in saddle bags." [8] Indian versions of the action in which General Custer and five companies were wiped out, state that when the horses of several troops were stampeded, the soldiers withdrew on foot firing revolvers.[9] Against a couple of thousand warriors, 18 rounds did not last long. Much carbine ammunition was evidently lost with the horses, and in any event the single shot .45-70 Springfields were no match in the open against the Spencers, Henrys and Sharps of so many mounted Indians.[10] General George Crook, reporting his repulse on the Rosebud by the same Indians, observed with understandable exaggeration: [11]

When the Sioux Indian was armed with a bow and arrow he was more formidable, fighting as he does most of the time on

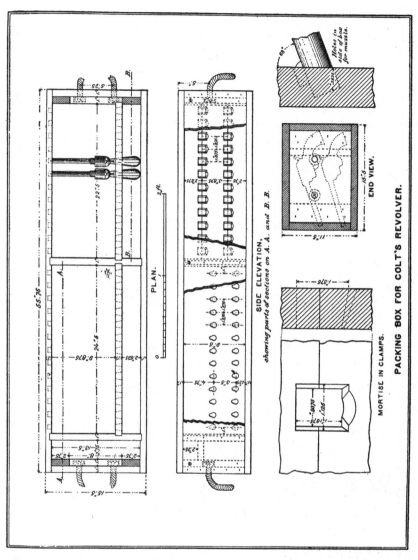

PLAN.

SIDE ELEVATION,
showing parts of sections on A. A. and B. B.

END VIEW.

MORTISE IN CLAMPS.

PACKING BOX FOR COLT'S REVOLVER.

Plan from Ordnance Memoranda, No. 22

horseback, than when he got the old fashioned muzzle-loading rifle. But when he came into possession of the breech-loader and metallic cartridge, which allows him to load and fire from his horse with perfect ease, he became at once ten thousand times more formidable.

With the improved arms, I have seen our friendly Indians, riding at full speed, shoot and kill a wolf, also on the run, while it it a rare thing that our troops can hit an Indian on horseback, though the soldier may be on his feet at the time. The Sioux is a cavalry soldier from the time he has intelligence enough to ride a horse or fire a gun.

An interesting insight into the survival rate of the single actions in the hands of the Army is afforded by the numbers which were repaired for the Government at the Colt factory from time to time after the model was superseded. In 1895-6 two thousand were returned for refinishing, of which only 23 were condemned at the factory. During the process some 1,200 of this lot had their barrels cut off to 5½ inch length. In 1901-2 another consignment of about 2,600 "5½ inch barrel S.A. Army Revolvers" were repaired and refinished, some 550 of these being shipped direct to Manila, for use in the Philippine Insurrection. A final lot of 2,600 were cleaned and repaired at the Colt factory in 1903 and returned to the Springfield Armory.

The serial numbers of these pistols indicate that very few appeared in more than one lot, so that an overall number of 7,000 or 19% may be considered accurate for the amount remaining on hand in 1903 of the 37,000 originally purchased by the Ordnance Department. In all three lots there were included revolvers from the first order of 8,000 procured in 1874 and issued while the Indian fighting was still going on. Of these the rate of survival was as follows:

Serial Nos.	Survival Rate, %
1 to 1,000	12.3
1,001 to 2,000	12.4
2,001 to 3,000	13.1
3,001 to 4,000	13.4
4,001 to 5,000	14.2
5,001 to 6,000	14.3
6,001 to 7,000	18.9
7,001 to 8,000	19.2

It is interesting to note that there were collectors of pistols even in those days with a penchant for low serials. Only one of the arms returned for refinishing had a number under 100, with two others under 200.

III

THE SCHOFIELD
SMITH & WESSON

MESSRS. SMITH & WESSON and Major Schofield did not permit themselves to be dis-
couraged by the initial adverse reports on their pistols. Early
in 1874 an ordnance board consisting of Major James G.
Benton, Commandant of the Springfield Armory, Captain
Edie and Lieutenant Henry Metcalfe was assembled by order
of the new Chief of Ordnance, Brigadier General Steven Vincent Benét, to examine further samples. Major Schofield was
permitted to attend almost every meeting of this board,
which began with a trial of two Smith & Wesson revolvers,
one of which resembled the Russian Model, of which some
200,000 had been ordered by the Tsar's Government. Two
distinctive features of the latter, added at the behest of Russian ordnance officers, were a knuckle or prawl at the top of
the handle and a spur or extra finger-hold on the triggerguard. The other sample submitted by Smith & Wesson was
not identified beyond the fact that it had a "new handle."
Both pistols passed firing, sanding and rust tests, but the
board reported on March 10, 1874, after calling attention to
undesirable particulars, viz:[1]

1. The shape of the handle, which makes the pistol hard to
cock and inconvenient to fire;
2. The shape of the comb of the hammer, which does not afford
a good hold to the thumb, . . .

28

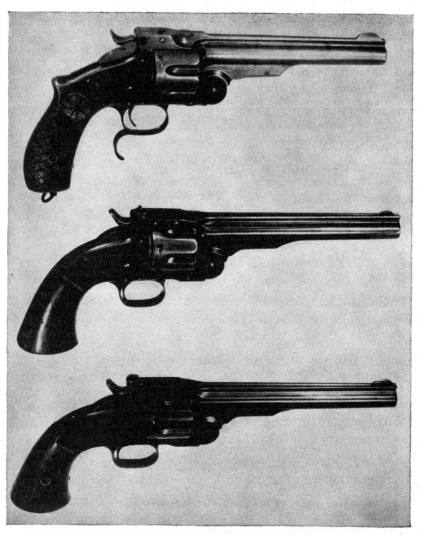

Smith & Wesson Russian and two Schofield Models

Photograph courtesy of Winchester Repeating Arms Company

3. The presence of the safety-lip and notch in the barrel-catch and frame respectively, which are more likely to cause accident than to prevent it . . .

4. That the extra finger-brace on the Russian model pistol offers no advantages to compensate for its evident inconvenience;

5. That the pistol is heavier than the Colt's pistol now in use;

6. That some of the original objections to this pistol, as regards the multiplicity and delicacy of parts, and the difficulty of assembling them, have not yet been overcome;

.   .   .   .

Resolved, That the Smith & Wesson pistols before the Board are not of a pattern well suited to the military service, and that the Board do not recommend the placing of any number of them in the hands of troops for trial in the field.

Major Schofield next presented his modification of the Smith & Wesson Russian Model, and this time met with a favorable reception. In this alteration the cylinder stop was arranged so as to allow ready removal of the cylinder, his patented form of ejector was simplified as to number of parts, the comb of the hammer made more concave in front, its safety lip ground off, and the handle knuckle reduced. It is probable that the trigger spur was also eliminated. After firing and rusting tests the board on April 22, 1874:

Resolved, That Major Schofield's alteration of Smith & Wesson's revolver, in consequence of its simplicity, efficiency, strength, lightness, and the ease with which it can be taken apart; and of the probability that its peculiar construction will diminish the cost of its manufacture below that of the Smith & Wesson pistol, is well suited for use in the military service. . . .

Major Schofield had a completely new specimen of his design ready in June for test by the board, on which Lieutenant George D. Ramsay, Jr. had meanwhile relieved Captain Edie. The new model embodied all the commended features of the alteration, and in addition the Schofield

patent barrel-latch, and a return to the American Model
style of grip, with complete elimination of the knuckle.
After a series of firings, in the course of which Major Schofield was freely permitted to make repairs and adjustments,
a trial of loading on horseback was conducted in comparison
with the Colt .45. At a hard gallop an expert horseman was
able to eject six empty shells and reload the Schofield with
cartridges taken from a belt pouch in 26 seconds, the Colt
requiring 60. This advantage was noted by the board in its
conclusions of June 30, 1874, as follows:

1. That the shapes of the handle and of the comb of the hammer of the Schofield pistol are better than those of the Smith &
Wesson;

2. That the parts of the pistol pertaining to the ejector,
cylinder-stay, and barrel-latch seem to be strong and simple, and
can be easily dismounted and replaced, and so far are considered
as improvements over the Smith & Wesson pistol;

3. It is thought that the barrel-latch of the Schofield pistol is
safer than that of the Smith & Wesson, in consequence of its
always being closed by the hammer before the piece is fired.

The weight of the pistol (2 lbs. 8¾ oz.) places it between the
Colt's (2 lbs. 5¾ oz.) and Smith & Wesson, old model (2 lbs. 10½
oz.). A portion of this difference is due to the length of barrel,
which in these pistols is respectively 7", 7.5" and 8".

In consideration of the foregoing facts, and of the ease with
which the pistol can be loaded on horseback at high speed, it was

Resolved, That in the opinion of the Board, Major Schofield's
revolver is well suited for the military service, and that the Board
do recommend that a limited number of these pistols be placed
in the hands of troops for comparative trial with the Colt's and
Smith & Wesson revolvers now in service, and that, as far as possible, the different pistols be tried side by side in the same commands.

The report of the board, submitted with the recommendation of the Chief of Ordnance that 3,000 Schofields be pur-

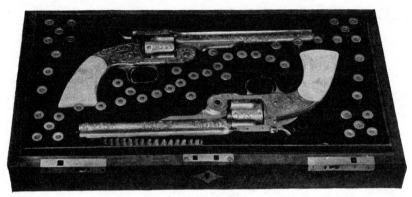

Cased Pair of Schofield Smith & Wessons which belonged to General Amaro Pombo, on the staff of President Porfirio Diaz of Mexico

chased, was approved by the Secretary of War on July 3, 1874. They were chambered for the .45 calibre centerfire cartridge with 28 grains of black powder and a bullet of 230 grains. An order for an additional lot was subsequently placed, these having a base pin with a longer bearing surface, a trigger with less curve, and a checkered and altered barrel-latch. This second model was tested at the Springfield Arsenal by Captain J. P. Farley. His report of January 12, 1876, stated that the modifications were proposed by Mr. Wesson with Major Schofield's acquiescence. The interest of this officer, whose brother, Major General John M. Schofield, had been Secretary of War in 1868, seems always to have commanded respectful attention from the Ordnance Department. With another veteran officer, Major General William B. Franklin, U.S.V., for vice-president and general manager, Colt's had satisfactory contacts too. Reports of the Ordnance Department indicate that in the fiscal year ending June 30, 1876, 3,000 Schofields were procured; in 1877, 5,003 and in 1878, two. Only parts for this model were subsequently purchased. The record of issues to Regular Army units was as follows: [2]

1876	859
1877	2,695
1878	182
1879	169
1880	331
1881	210
1882	35
1883	226
1884	24
1885	—
1886	24
1887	38
1888	—
1889	146
1890	28
1891	31
1892	17
1893	3
Total	5,019

As in the case of the Colt, the Schofield was also issued by the Ordnance Department to the militia, in the total amount of 3,569. Consequently, it is apparent that some of the latter arms were second hand. While the Schofield evidently had its devotees in the Army, its popularity was nothing like as great nor as enduring as that of the Colt. Preference among the military was reflected in the annual report for 1877 of the ordnance officer attached to the command most active against the Indians. Thus Captain Otho Ernest Michaelis, of the Department of Dakota, wrote: [3]

The experience of the past year, has shown that the Colt's calibre .45 pistol is a reliable weapon. The Schofield Smith and Wesson Revolvers used in the field, have not proved themselves acceptable to Cavalry officers.

Of course their only claim to superiority over the Colt's, is founded upon their capability of automatic extraction. This feature, however, is attained at the expense of simplicity of mechanism and strength.

. . . That Cavalry officers themselves do not pay much attention to the quality of rapid ejection is proven by the fact that they
do not desire to carry on the person, more than twelve rounds of
ammunition. In the pistol charge of the battalion of the Seventh
Cavalry upon the Nez Perces position on Snake Creek,[4] Captain
Godfrey informs me that his men fired only a single round. . . .
Instances have been reported to me of the Schofield Smith and
Wesson barrel-catch's being drawn back while in the holster, and
the cartridges being, in consequence, ejected in drawing the
weapon.

Captain Michaelis himself was an enthusiast for the self-
cocking revolver, which because of its rapidity of fire he pre-
dicted would become "the future pistol of the army." In
1877 he had been carrying a new .38 Colt double action
"Lightning," and recommended it as deserving of trial.

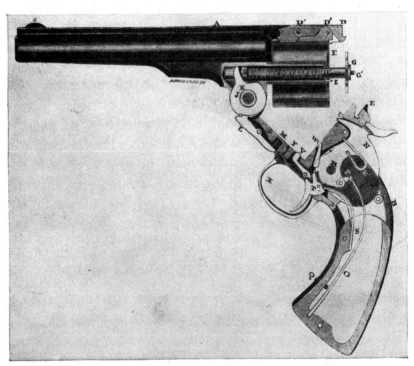

Diagram of Schofield from Ordnance Memoranda, No. 22

Advertisements of B. Kittredge & Co. commencing in September, 1877,[5] listed the ".45 Smith & Wesson, Army" for sale at $16 (later $15) with nickel plating $1 extra, but there is no cut to indicate which model was offered. Apart from a few presentation arms found in Mexico, this is the single indication known that the Schofield was manufactured for commercial sale. Smith & Wesson's own advertisements of the period show only their Russian model in .44 calibre and a smaller .38 arm.[6] A possible explanation why the Schofield model was not further developed or exploited may lie in the inventor's untimely death. He took his life with his own pistol at Fort Apache, Arizona, on December 17, 1882. An obituary in *The New York Herald*[7] states that "he had been crazed for eight or ten days over some invention of his, and it is supposed that in a moment of temporary insanity he shot himself." Schofield revolvers were offered for sale to the public in the 1892 catalog of Hartley & Graham at $13.50, but the fact that they were of the first model, with uncheckered barrel-latch, indicates that they came from the original Army order of 3,000. A number of these are believed to have been bought by the American Express Co. to arm their employees, and are sometimes found nickel-plated with barrels shortened to five inches.

IV

THE REMINGTON MODEL OF 1875

MUCH of the foregoing history is reviewed in Ordnance Notes, No. LIV, which may be found in the *Army and Navy Journal* of February 10, 1877,[1] as well as in the official volume. They also record the proceedings of a board of officers consisting of Captain J. P. Farley and Lieutenant James Rockwell, Jr., convened at the Springfield Arsenal on February 23, 1876, to pass on the merits of the Remington .44 calibre Model of 1875 as compared with the Peacemaker and Schofield. The board decided at the outset that "in view of the fact that no comparative trial or record has as yet been made between the Colt or Schofield," it would be necessary to institute the same trial for all three revolvers. A series of tests were devised which thereafter became standard. Excellent section drawings of the pistols by C. A. Emery, draughtsman of the Springfield Armory are reproduced herein, as is likewise the table of dimensions and weights on page 38.

The results of firing tests are also given in tabular form, except for deviation, where differences were negligible. In rapidity of loading and ejecting, the Schofield took only 59 seconds to fire 18 shots, commencing and ending with chambers empty. Time for the Colt was 1 minute, 54 seconds, and for the Remington approximately the same, after allowing for a misfire. Other tests are given on page 39.

36

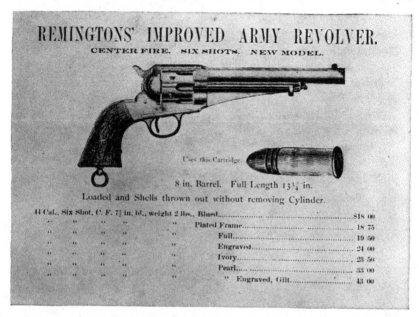

REMINGTONS' IMPROVED ARMY REVOLVER.

CENTER FIRE. SIX SHOTS. NEW MODEL.

Use this Cartridge.

8 in. Barrel. Full Length 13¾ in.

Loaded and Shells thrown out without removing Cylinder.

44 Cal., Six Shot, C. F. 7¼ in. bl., weight 2 lbs., Blued	$18 00
" " " " " Plated Frame	18 75
" " " " " Full	19 50
" " " " " Engraved	24 00
" " " " " Ivory	28 50
" " " " " Pearl	33 00
" " " " " Engraved, Gilt	43 00

From Remington Price List, 1877

Courtesy of the Bella C. Landauer Collection in The New-York Historical Society

The dusting test consisted of firing twelve rounds after the revolvers were shaken in fine dust, then roughly brushed. Six more rounds were fired after a second dusting. The Colt worked freely. The Schofield loaded with difficulty after the second application. The ejector of the Remington bound, and it took much force to push the cartridges into the chambers for the final firing. When the pistols were dismounted a vise was required to extract the fouled center pin of the Colt. For dismounting every part it took an ordinary machinist 5 minutes for the Colt, 7½ for the Schofield and 7 for the Remington. In the same order, assembly required 17, 19 and 24 minutes, the greater time for the Remington being due to delay in slipping the main spring into place.

The rusting tests of this trial consisted in dipping the revolvers in a solution of sal ammoniac for ten minutes and

	Colt	Schofield	Remington
DIMENSIONS:			
Total length, inches	12.5	12.5	13.03
Length of barrel, inches	7.5	7	7.46
Diameter of bore, inches	0.45	0.435	0.44
Grooves, depth, inches	0.005	0.0075	0.004
Grooves, number of	6	5	5
Twist	Left	Right	Left
Uniform, one turn in inches . .	16	20	
At base, one turn in inches . .			5
At muzzle, one turn in inches . .			26
WEIGHTS:			
Total weight, pounds	2.31	2.5	2.6
Weight of powder charge, grains . .	28	28	28.3
Weight of bullet, grains	230	230	226.6

	Initial Velocity, ft.	Pene-tration	Recoil
FIRING TESTS:			
Schofield, service ammunition . . .	744	46	57
Colt, service ammunition	733	47	56
Colt, Bridgeport ammunition * . . .	890	58	74
Remington, Remington ammunition .	655	43	53

* 37.6 grs. powder, 249.6 grs. lead.

---

then exposing them for forty-eight hours. After firing twelve rounds, the process was repeated. The results were relatively favorable to the Colt, and least favorable to the Schofield, which loaded and ejected with difficulty in the first test and could not be fired at all after the second rusting. As between the Colt and Remington, both worked at first without difficulty, but required the cylinder to be forced around in the second instance. The ejector of the Remington stuck when forced in the chamber, and its trigger bound. Full details of the tests are given in an excerpt from Ordnance Notes, No. LIV, reproduced in Haven & Belden, previously cited.

ENDURANCE

Two hundred and fifty rounds were then fired from each revolver, allowing them a short time to cool after every fifty rounds.

The Colt worked without the least difficulty.

The Schofield Smith and Wesson clogged slightly in the cylinder after the 180th round, but the clogging did not increase.

The Remington clogged in the cylinder at the 162d round, and worked with some difficulty thereafter. . . .

FOULING

The revolvers were then allowed to remain forty-eight hours uncleaned, after which 50 rounds were fired from each, allowing the arm to cool after the 12th, 24th, and 36th rounds.

The Colt revolver was considerably fouled, but worked without difficulty.

The Schofield Smith and Wesson was also considerably fouled, but worked without difficulty.

The Remington appeared less badly fouled than the two others. In firing the first 6 rounds the cylinder did not revolve readily. From the 12th to the 18th round both hands were required to hold the revolver in cocking. In firing the last 14 rounds the base pin stuck somewhat, due to the fouling of the front of the cylinder about the base pin. . . .

Drawings shown illustrate the mechanical differences noted in the revolvers. Emphasis was put upon the single forging of the butt and frame of the Remington, the double finger of the Colt hand whose more extended action allowed the ratchet to be cut in a larger circle, and the necessity of exact and invariable dimensions in the less rigid system of the Schofield. The board found no improvement over the Colt in the light base pin of the Remington, its ejector housing, nor in placing the ejector spring around the base pin instead

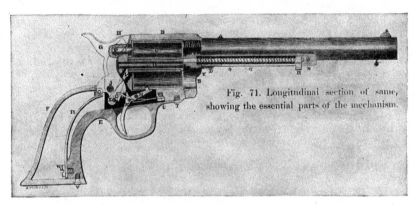

Diagram of Colt from Ordnance Memoranda, No. 22

of the ejector rod. In conclusion, the board, adverting to the simplicity, stability and endurance of the Colt, expressed a "decided preference" for it as the arm "best adapted to meet all the requirements of the military service." The potential of the arm using the commercial instead of the service cartridge was emphasized, and its ejector was deemed to have as much rapidity as required for a weapon of its purpose. In competition with it, the points of difference in the Remington were found to "fall so far short of improvements as to condemn the arm for the military service." As to the Scho-

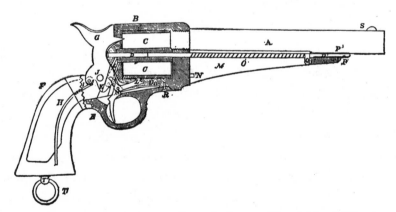

Diagram of Remington from Ordnance Notes, No. LIV

field, the board, after noting it was already in service, and again mentioning the rusting test, expressed the view that its workmanship, fine adjustment and ingenuity of mechanism would make it "in demand by a large class of commissioned officers in time of war." It was the first model of Schofield, already issued to troops, that was subjected to the test.

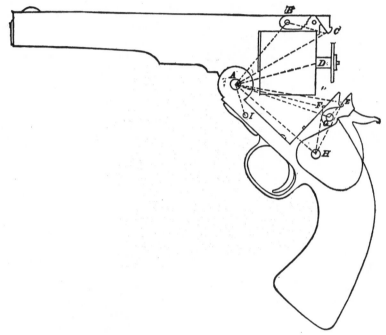

Diagram of Schofield from Ordnance Notes, No. LIV

This report was submitted by the Acting Chief of Ordnance to the Secretary of War, who gave it his approval on June 28, 1876. The Colt single action continued to be an official arm of the cavalry service until 1892, and was also adopted in a 5½ inch barrel length for artillery use. No more than 8,005 Schofields were ordered by the Government, but several authorities assert that a number of the Remington Model of 1875 were also purchased and issued.[2] This is not substantiated by the Annual Reports of the Chief of Ordnance nor have any Remingtons come to the notice of the author in .45 calibre or stamped "U. S." to indicate Government issue. It seems anomalous that the Army would issue Remingtons in .44 calibre, when the service cartridge for both the Colt and Schofield was .45, but .44 is the bore given by the

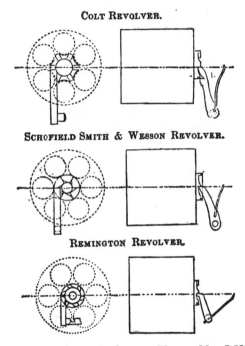

COLT REVOLVER.

SCHOFIELD SMITH & WESSON REVOLVER.

REMINGTON REVOLVER.

Diagrams from Ordnance Notes, No. LIV

aforesaid authorities for those supposed to have been purchased. The Remington Model of 1875 was of course advertised and sold commercially, and 10,000 of them in .44 calibre were purchased by the Egyptian Government.[3]

The negative conclusion reached in the foregoing paragraph is supported by collateral evidence of two kinds. First is the fact that a Model 1875 Remington of service calibre was actually tested at Springfield in 1877.[4] In order to accommodate the .45 cartridge the diameter of the cylinder was increased ¹⁄₁₆ of an inch. The trial, by a board composed of Captain George W. McKee and Lieutenant John E. Greer, was ordered by the Chief of Ordnance because of exceptions taken to the published report of the previous test. On the statement therein that "the Remington revolver does not differ essen-

COLT REVOLVER.

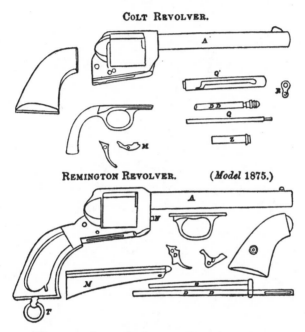

REMINGTON REVOLVER.   (*Model* 1875.)

Diagrams from Ordnance Notes, No. LIV

tially in principle from the Colt," W. S. Smoot, Superintendent of E. Remington & Sons, commented:

In as much as the frame of the Colt revolver, upon which much stress is laid in the earlier portion of the report, has only recently been changed to conform to that characteristic of our own for many years, we think this remark uncalled for, and it is an important question as to whether, the minor details of our arm has been derived from the Colt, or whether, both have been derived from earlier forms.

This criticism was met by the trial board with the observation "the fact remains that there is a strong resemblance between them." The board applied the same tests as previously except for using a stronger solution of sal ammoniac. Results of the rusting test were less favorable than before. The hammer cocked with the greatest difficulty, the base pin could not be withdrawn by hand, the loading gate had to be pried open with a screw-driver, and the ejector rod could only be moved with a hammer. In the face of these findings the conclusion that "on the whole the Board regards this as an excellent service revolver" was but faint praise.

The second point of evidence is a monograph on *The Fabrication of Small Arms for United States Service* by Lieutenant Colonel James G. Benton, published in 1878 as Ordnance Memoranda, No. 22. In the section devoted to handarms the Colt and Schofield only are mentioned, together with detailed instructions for their inspection and testing.[5] This publication identifies the various stampings to be found on Government issue arms of these makes as follows:

COLT MODEL OF 1873:
1. "U. S." on lower frame, left side.
2. Proof letter "P":
    (a) on barrel, underside just forward of center pin;
    (b) on cylinder, 0.2″ from rear on center line of a groove.
3. Subinspector's initials:
    (a) on frame just forward of serial number;
    (b) on barrel just in rear of proofmark;
    (c) on cylinder 0.2″ from rear on center line of a groove;
    (d) on stock 0.1″ from butt, right side (also on left as receiving stamp if subinspector receives arm).
4. If inspected by an officer, his initials as receiving stamp on stock 0.1″ from butt, left side, and year of inspection above such initials.
5. Letter "C" stamped on all condemned parts.

SCHOFIELD SMITH & WESSON

1. "U. S." on butt of frame.
2. Proof letter "P":
    (a) on barrel underside projection, right side;
    (b) on cylinder 0.1" from rear in center line of a groove.
3. Subinspector's initials:
    (a) on frame, right side;
    (b) on barrel just forward of proofmarks;
    (c) on cylinder 0.1" from rear in center line of a groove;
    (d) on stock, same as with Colt.
4. If inspected by an officer, same as with Colt.
5. Letter "C" stamped on all condemned parts.

V

CONTEMPORARY OPINIONS

WHILE the comparative trials of 1876 were going on, the *Army and Navy Journal* published an editorial [1] outlining the main points of difference between the cartridge Colt and the old cap-and-ball model. This was before the *Journal* had carried any advertising of the new design, but copy on a substantial scale was soon to follow. The comparison read:

This is the simplest cartridge revolver made, everything being plain and strong. It differs from the old one in having a solid frame for the cylinder, like the Remington revolver. The hand which revolves the cylinder has two fingers, giving a gain of power and diminishing the chance of breakage in hard service. The ejector is like the old rammer, but slides up and down in a tube instead of working with a lever. A spiral spring takes it back after each shell is ejected. The provision for loading is very simple, a piece of the breech, called "the gate," ejecting outward with a thumb piece, and closing again. The cylinder is, of course, open at both ends, like other metallic cartridge revolvers. The shells are central fire, and can be reloaded, like rifle shells.

A conclusion drawn in the editorial that the new Colt "has beaten all competitors and stands today at the head of all the cartridge pistols as the Army weapon, *par excellence*" was promptly challenged by a correspondent [2] signing himself "Veritas." He pointed out that the Schofield revolver was initially ordered "notwithstanding the fact that the Government had already . . . bought enough Colts to arm the entire

46

cavalry force." A further assertion was that as far as the number would go, the Schofield had "entirely superseded the Colt, giving unbounded satisfaction."

Publication the next year of Ordnance Notes No. LIV generated far more heat among the respective partisans of the Peacemaker and Schofield, who fought an inconclusive battle of words in the correspondence columns of the *Army and Navy Journal.* In the April 7, 1877, issue there is quoted a letter from a Schofield enthusiast characterizing the board's report as "so manifestly one-sided and unjust in its conclusions that it should not be suffered to pass without some attempt at criticism." After questioning the relevancy of the better showing of Colt's Bridgeport ammunition "in penetration of pine butts," the writer defended the jointed frame system of the Schofield as follows: [3]

What the board claims as a defect is the great distinguishing feature of the Schofield, Smith and Wesson, which makes it superior to all other revolvers now in use. By its peculiar construction all the empty shells are ejected at once, leaving the chambers exposed ready for reloading without going through the tedious operation of punching them out one by one, as is the case with the Colt.

He then adverted to the rapidity of loading and ejecting test and to the horseback trial made in 1873, in both of which the Schofield excelled. As for the rusting and fouling tests conducted at the Springfield Armory, his opinion was that no revolver should ever be subjected to such abuse and that comparison of it with conditions resulting from exposure and use in the field could be "characterized only as an unmitigated fudge."

A defense of the findings of the board was not long in making its appearance. On April 21st a correspondent sign-

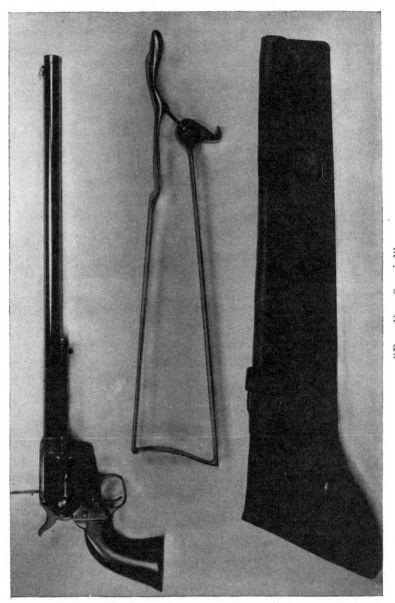

"Buntline Special"

Courtesy of John S. du Mont

ing himself "Pine Butts" commented on the ejecting speed of the Schofield: [4]

. . . Suppose only 4 or 3 or 2, or, what is perhaps more frequently the case in real frontier use, only one chamber has been discharged. Then the Smith and Wesson extractor must of necessity displace *all the loaded* shells to displace the *one* discharged. . . . How much time has been saved and how much is the advantage now?

Will this offset the advantage of a *solid* frame?—fewer parts, no hinge to rust or wear loose, no catch or catch spring to get out of order—*a solid frame.*

Another writer entered the lists on May 26 under the pseudonym "Barrel Latch" with the statement: [5]

There are no Smith and Wesson revolvers proper, in the hands of United States troops. A few were purchased several years ago for trial [the American Model], but were universally objected to because some of the parts were too delicate and because the mechanism was too complicated. The "system" was universally liked and . . . it was only necessary to correct, simplify, and strengthen the working parts to make it a great success. This was done by an inventor previously unknown as such who after over three years of study and labor presented the Army with the Schofield-Smith and Wesson revolver, which was promptly recognized by the Ordnance Department . . . although the same Department had repeatedly rejected the Smith and Wesson "regular" and the "Russian Smith and Wesson."

It remained for General Sherman to express, however inadvertently, an authoritative preference between the several makes in a letter to Lieutenant General Sheridan on February 20, 1878. Discussing generally changes in military equipment, the Commanding General wrote: "I think our infantry soldier should be armed with the best rifle, a Colt's revolver, and a knife. . . . The rifle and revolver should use the same identical cartridge." The latter was a favorite though military-wise unorthodox view of General Sherman's, then finding an exemplification in the .44-40 cartridge for which the frontier version of the Colt and the Model 1873 Winchester rifle were both chambered. Lieutenant General Sheridan replied April 5th after consultation with Captain J. W. Reilly of the Ordnance Department, whose views he annexed. General Sheridan wrote: "The Cavalry wants, first, a good horse, a good Springfield rifle . . . then a good revolving pistol, and a knife. . . . I am not in favor of a pistol for infantry. . . . I doubt if pistols can be made to shoot the rifle cartridge; it contains too much powder, and the recoil would be too great." [6] The general was evidently unaware that the combination had been effected in the Austrian military revolver, which took the same cartridge as the Werndl rifle and carbine, the powder charge being however reduced with the space left vacant filled by a wad. [7]

The most novel suggestion of all was put forward by Captain Reilly—that every soldier should be issued a few cartridges loaded with buckshot, for close-in work. This was taken up by a corresponent of the *Army and Navy Journal* signing himself "Cavalryman" in the May 18th issue, whose comment seems to have laid at rest, in that periodical at least, the controversy between partisans of the several makes: [8]

The "Colts improved" and the Smith and Wesson Schofield improved, are both good, both have their advocates, and no serious complaints can be brought against either, and I think that in a fight one is just as good as the other, and do as much execution; but the pistol for a Cavalryman is the one suggested by Capt. J. W. Reilly, Ord. Dept., viz. a pistol that will throw buck shot— or buck and ball.

A comparison of the Peacemaker and Schofield contemporaneous with their initial appearance is to be found in the reports of the judges at the Centennial Exposition of 1876

Colt's Exhibit at the Philadelphia Centennial of 1876

Courtesy of Colt's Manufacturing Company

held at Philadelphia.[9] Both arms were exhibited at this international fair by their respective makers, and both awarded commendations. The single action Colt was likewise included by the U. S. Ordnance Department in its exhibit of the latest equipment and arms of a cavalryman.[10] In the general report of the firearms judges the previous history of military revolvers was summarized as follows:

The invention of the Colt revolving pistol, in 1836, was the first giving any promise of success as a military weapon of this class. Its performances during the Mexican War, in 1847, were far from satisfactory, but by a series of improvements it was brought, by the year 1857, to a pretty high degree of efficiency. It performed a conspicuous part in the War of the Rebellion, where it was very generally used in the cavalry service. Many other revolvers, in principle like the Colt, were put forward during this war. In 1867 the Colt was transformed to use metallic cartridges, and is now one of the adopted arms of the cavalry service. The Smith & Wesson revolver, using metallic cartridges, has also been and is now very considerably used in the cavalry service.

While Major Schofield's name was not mentioned either in the report or in the exhibit, it is probable from the context that his was one of the military models exhibited by Smith & Wesson, as to whose product the award read:

Commended for its capacity as a military arm. The ejection of all the discharged shells simultaneously, the workmanship and materials used in its manufacture, its interchangeability, and the simplicity of its action, render it a desirable weapon for defense or offense.

E. Remington & Sons also had exhibits at the Exposition which were commended, but the reports indicate that these were long arms rather than revolvers. Of Colt's display, the judges evidently had in mind the Peacemaker when they observed:

A military weapon extracting the discharged shells singly; combining strength and simplicity of action; not liable to get out of order; readily taken apart and easily cleaned; having entire exchangeability of parts, with a high order of finish. Commended for durability and actual service in the hands of a soldier. . . .

The preference of frontiersmen for the single action Colt and the reasons controlling their choice were clearly put by A. C. Gould, one of the early authorities on American handarms writing from the shooter's viewpoint. In the first edition, published in 1888, of his *Modern American Pistols and Revolvers* the ample strength of the Colt and its ability to stand rough usage were contrasted with the delicacy of parts of other makes. Without expressing any personal preference, Mr. Gould reached the conclusion that "the combined points of the solid frame and the arm being unaffected, so far as operating it is concerned, by neglecting to clean it while using or afterwards, has made the Colt's revolver the chosen arm of many frontiersmen. . . ."

This opinion was shared by Theodore Roosevelt, an observer whose objectivity was quite beyond question. He wrote in 1885 from his ranch on the Little Missouri in Dakota Territory: [11] "Of course every ranchman carries a revolver, a long 45 Colt or Smith & Wesson, by preference the former." In another context he observed:

The revolver was formerly a necessity to protect the owner from Indians and other human foes; this is still the case in a few places, but, as a rule, it is now carried merely from habit, or to kill rattlesnakes, or on the chance of falling in with a wolf or coyote, while not infrequently it is used to add game to the cowboy's not too varied bill of fare.

It is interesting to note that in the equestrian statue of Roosevelt standing in front of the Natural History Museum in New York City, he is wearing a pair of holstered revolvers

which by the flare of their butts are unmistakably Peacemakers.

An even more positive expression of the general preference
is to be found in the correspondence columns of *The Field*
in 1884.[12] Introduction in England of a new model of Webley
double action military revolver made its comparison with the

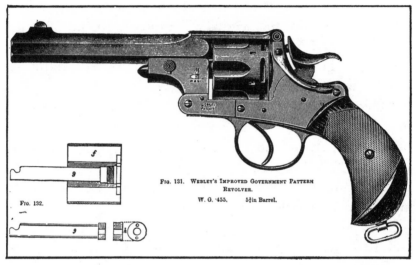

FIG. 131. WEBLEY'S IMPROVED GOVERNMENT PATTERN
REVOLVER.

W. G. ·455,   5⅛in Barrel.

FIG. 132.

From Walsh, *The Modern Sportsman's Gun and Rifle,* 1884

American cavalry pistol a timely topic. Each weapon had its
enthusiasts, but no one challenged the assertion of a correspondent that the Colt single action "is the special weapon
of the American Cavalry, and of hunters, trappers, cowboys,
ranchmen and miners on the frontier, who may be credited
with knowing what a revolver should be, and who generally
prefer this pistol to Colt's or Smith Wesson's double action
pistols." The discussion led to a trial of the Webley, fired by
its inventor, on the target range at Nunhead, followed by a
test of the Colt single and double actions, fired by the cele-
brated pistolshot Ira Paine. As reported in *The Field,* "His

shooting at 12 yards was certainly better, but he did not come up to Mr. H. Webley's 25 yards diagram." At 50 yards, a distance at which Webley did not shoot, Paine's "six shots made a square of 18 inches or thereabouts."

Another interesting comparison between the Colt and the Webley was made by Major W. McClintock, R. A., Assistant Superintendent of the Royal Small Arms Factory at Enfield, who measured the recoil of these pistols. He found that the .44-40 Colt, with a charge of 40 grains of powder and a 200 grain bullet, had a recoil of 4.966 foot pounds, whereas the Webley .455 with 18 grains powder and 265 grains lead, recorded 4.814. Major McClintock's remarks were quoted in *The Field* as follows: [13]

It may be supposed that, owing to its large powder charge, the recoil of the Colt's Frontier revolver is excessive; but this is not so. As a matter of fact . . . the recoil of this pistol is little more than that of revolvers firing the Government 0.455 cartridge; and, on account of the balance of the Frontier pistol, even this slight excess of recoil is not felt by the firer.

This comparison was probably made to refute an assertion of John Henry Walsh, the reporter of the trial at Nunhead, that the recoil of Colt's .44 was "very heavy" and "only bearable to men of very strong physique." [14] Major McClintock's attitude may also be contrasted with that of the Surveyor General of Ordnance, to whom Colt's London agency submitted a specimen of the Peacemaker in 1877. The arm was sent back by the War Office with the comment that it "has been carefully examined" but "is not considered equal to the service revolver" (then the Adams double action). Baron Von Oppen reported rather bitterly to his home office that the "pistol has been returned to us without a single cartridge having been fired out of it."

VI

MULTIBALL CARTRIDGES

THE suggestion, previously noted, of Captain Reilly for the development of a multiball cartridge was soon taken up by an ordnance officer at the Frankfort Arsenal. On June 13, 1878, Captain E. M. Wright reported that he had altered a .45 Colt's revolver to take such a load, which would also fit the Springfield rifle and carbine.[1] The pistol was modified by increasing the length of the cylinder and frame and reducing the chambers to five, the resulting increase in weight being only six ounces. The new cartridge was long enough to hold from forty to fifty-five grains of powder and three round balls of buckshot one behind the other. Captain Wright also experimented with bullets cut into horizontal segments but found them unsatisfactory. He fired his altered Colt from a fixed rest and reported that with 45 grains of powder the recoil averaged 34 pounds and penetration in boards at 25 yards was 2.7 inches for all three balls. This compared with 21 pounds recoil and 3.9 inches penetration for the ordinary service ammunition. The muzzle velocity of the 45 grain multiball charge was 741 feet per second as compared to 732. Ten buckshot charges fired from a rest at 25 yards distance hit within a circle 12 inches across, the diameter for a service revolver and ammunition being 7 inches.

When this report was forwarded to the Commandant of the Springfield Arsenal for comment, Colonel Benton recommended a service trial of the new ammunition for the rifle and carbine, but observed with notable candor:

The changes proposed, of increasing the weight of the revolver and reducing the number of chambers in the cylinder to enable it to carry the same cartridge as the rifle and carbine, seem to me objectionable and not warranted by the good to be obtained. The revolver being intended for hand-to-hand combat, should, in my opinion, not have long range unless this can be obtained without sacrificing lightness, and without reducing its number of charges.

DESCRIPTION OF BUCKSHOT CARTRIDGE, FOR PRESENT SERVICE ARMS AND ALTERED REVOLVERS.—CAL. .45 BUCKSHOT.

Case, present rifle case, uniformly tapered; charge, 40 or 45 grains service powder; 3 round bullets, pure lead; diameter, ".458; lubricant, bullets dipped in Japan wax, bullets pushed in far enough to afford a good crimp on last one.

Capt. Wright's first design, from Report of Chief of Ordnance, 1879

Captain Wright had meanwhile busied himself with the development of other multiball cartridges, one containing two balls that would fit the Colt and Schofield Smith & Wesson without their being altered, and a second with three balls that would fit only the Colt, provided its chambers were reamed a bit where they were choked at the forward end. These cartridges were loaded with 20 to 25 grains of powder, and their inventor claimed for them sufficient penetration and a recoil about the same as with service ammunition. Trial of these cartridges at the Springfield Armory is reflected in the annual report of the Chief of Ordnance for 1879, which stated: [2]

I append a series of reports on the multiball cartridge for revolver. For use in the rifle and carbine, it has not been received with favor, the reports from the field being almost unanimously against it.

Its efficiency as a revolver cartridge will depend on its results at very short ranges—certainly within 25 yards—and on the extent of its scattering.

I quote from report of Captain Greer, Ordnance Department, a most capable and experienced officer and experimenter, made June 7, last:

"With regard to dispersion of fire, which is the true *raison d'être* of these cartridges, an inspection of the tables shows that at short ranges there is none at all, the bullet hole of each shot nearly coinciding. At longer ranges—75 to 100 yards—there is a considerable dispersion of balls; but they have too little power to do much execution."

The department will continue its endeavors to adapt this cartridge to the revolver, and it may be that some simple change in its arrangement and form may fulfill the conditions necessary to make it a success.

General Benét's determination to continue the experiment, despite the adverse opinion entertained at Springfield, was largely due to the enthusiasm for the multiball shown by yet another agency of the Army. An equipment board of line officers presided over by General Nelson A. Miles had met December 16, 1878, to consider among other items two patterns of smoothbore revolvers for firing multiball or buckshot cartridges—a self-cocking pistol presented by Remington & Co. of New York, and another by W. C. Dodge of Washington. The board's report in the *Army and Navy Journal* of August 9, 1879,[3] states that "while the mechanism of the pistols seem to be good their general merits were not fully tested by the Board. They were the means of demonstrating, however, that at effective distances the destructive power of the pistol is greatly increased by the 'multiball' or buckshot cartridges, and the Board is so much impressed with the value of that kind of ammunition that it recommends that it be manufactured and adapted to the Army Revolver."

In response to a directive to "get up a multiball cartridge for the Colt's *service* revolver," Captain Wright in August, 1879, devised a case which, to have sufficient length and yet pass the choke of the chamber, was slightly bottled at the forward end. This allowed the use of three bullets, diameter, .428; weight, 110 grains; charge of powder, 25 grains. The three balls were segments of spheres, the two extremes hav-

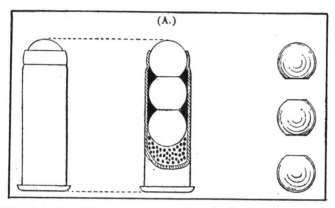

Capt. Wright's last design, from Report of Chief of Ordnance, 1879

ing one base, the middle having two. The powder was closely compressed, occupying but .42 inches of the case, which was 1.61 inches long.

Tested by a board of officers at Springfield consisting of Lieutenants Rogers Birnie, Jr., and C. C. Morrison, the new cartridge was found to have an initial velocity of 690 feet, a recoil nearly twice that of the service cartridge, penetration from 1.65 inches at 25 yards to .72 inches at 100, and mean deviation increasing greatly over the service cartridge beyond 25 yards distance. The conclusions of the board were reported as follows:

The efficiency of the cartridge turns upon two considerations: first, accuracy; second, effective energy.

MERWIN, HULBERT & Co's MULTIBALL CARTRIDGE.

FOR THE SERVICE RIFLE.

Fig. 1

Fig. 2.

Fig. 3.

Legend.

Weight of Powder charge,........ .... 52 grains.
Number of Balls in each Cartridge, 3.
Diameter of Balls,................ 0".424.
Weight of each Ball,..............108.66 grains.
Total Weight of Lead,.......... 326 grains.

FOR THE REVOLVER.

Fig. 4.

Fig. 5.

Fig. 6.

Legend.

Weight of Powder charge, ... 22 grains.
No. of Balls, (1 Ogival + 2 Sph! segments) 3.
Diameter of Balls,..................... 0".424.
Length of Ogival Bullet,.............. 0".39.
Altitude of Segments, ... 0".236.
Weight of Ogival Bullet,..... .... 111 grains.
　　do. ,, Segments, (each).......... 82　do.
Total Weight of Lead,............... 275　do.

From Report of Chief of Ordnance, 1879

In point of accuracy . . . the multiball cartridge is a little superior to the service up to 25 yards; between that and 50 yards, nearly twice that of the service against a front of men, and nearly equal . . . against a single file.

Between 50 and 100 yards it approaches nearly three times that of the service cartridge against a front of men.

The board finds the question of effectiveness a very serious one about which to arrive at a conclusion, with available data. Even at 50 yards, which they consider a minimum effective range for a revolver cartridge, the energy of one of the three bullets is scarcely more than one-third of that of the service bullet at the same range.

The experiments lead to the conclusion of a probable and marked superiority (on account of the greater number of balls) of the multiball cartridge over the service, to include a range of 50 yards; but even within this limit, it is believed a well-grounded conclusion can only be arrived at by actual trial in service, in order to determine the capability of the multiball bullet to inflict a dangerous or a fatal wound.

The board also stressed the loss of efficiency involved in using a .45 calibre rifled revolver for firing a relatively light .428 spherical bullet, the size of the latter being necessarily limited by the dimensions of the Colt chamber, and the cartridge not being usable in the Schofield Smith & Wesson at all.

Previously another board at Springfield consisting of Captain Greer and Lieutenant Birnie had tested an even less efficient multiball revolver cartridge submitted by Messrs. Merwin, Hulbert & Co. of New York. This cartridge, which contained 22 grains of powder, held three bullets .424 inches in diameter all enclosed in a lubricated paper casing, which in turn fitted into a copper cartridge case of service dimensions. The front ball was ogival, weighing 111 grains, the latter two spherical segments each of 82 grains. These characteristics made possible firing the cartridge from either the service Colt or Schofield, with a hitting effect, above 25 yards, equal to two and sometimes three uniball cartridges. However, the concussion given by a hit was thought to be far less than that of a single heavy bullet, the penetration at 25 yards being only 1.5 inches for the ogival section and from 1 to 1.25 inches for the other segments, and falling off greatly above that distance. It is interesting to note that the fouling was found to be very slight, the paper casing taking the rifling and being thrown off by centrifugal force after leaving the barrel.

The efforts of the Ordnance Department to develop a satisfactory multiball load for revolvers appear to have ended with the trials of the Merwin Hulbert cartridge and of the last of Captain Wright's designs. In 1879 the Department issued 9,000 multiball cartridges and in 1880 three hundred.[4] There were none issued thereafter, nor was the subject mentioned again in the reports of the Chief of Ordnance. A single later comment has been found in an article in *The Cavalry Journal* for 1888.[5] There Lieutenant Eben Swift of the 5th Cavalry took issue with the reasons advanced by the Ordnance Department for condemning the multiball cartridge. He considered that the experiments gave excellent results at seventy-five yards, a single cartridge doing the work of three so far as accuracy went, with just the right amount of dispersion. That distance was in his opinion the extreme limit at which revolvers should be used by mounted men. As for the lack of dispersion at twenty-five yards, Lieutenant Swift considered this fact an advantage rather than otherwise, because of the probability that "the battering effect of three bullets in the same place will be immensely greater than that of a single larger bullet." However questionable this premise, the opinion of the writer is entitled to respect. He was one of the few officers in the United States Army who later foresaw and protested the fatal loss of stopping power when the .45 revolver was superseded by the .38.[6]

VII

OTHER RIVALS

WITH the adoption of the Colt and Schofield as official arms of the United States Cavalry, they very soon became standards against which pistols of other makes were tested. In a previous chapter the Remington Model of 1875 was discussed, but even before it was submitted the Ordnance Department conducted trials of two revolvers made by Messrs. Forehand and Wadsworth. These gentlemen were sons-in-law and the successors of Ethan Allen, an arms manufacturer of Worcester, Massachusetts, who is perhaps best remembered for his revolving pepperboxes. Their pistols were submitted through Messrs. Schuyler, Hartley & Graham, arms dealers of New York City, and were tested at the Springfield Arsenal in December, 1874, pursuant to orders from the Chief of Ordnance directing a comparison with the Colt and Schofield.

The trial board consisted of Captain J. P. Farley and Lieutenant James Rockwell, Jr., the same officers who later tested the Remington. Their unpublished report, which was favorably endorsed and forwarded by Colonel Benton, is contained in the Springfield Armory Records at The National Archives.[1] The board was unable at that time to procure a sample of the Schofield, it being still in process of manufacture, so the test was made entirely against the Colt. The Forehand & Wadsworth revolvers had a solid frame, a hollow retractable center pin holding the cylinder in place, and an ejector rod which when not in use was seated inside this pin.

64

The rod also fitted through the shoulder of a ferrule turning around the barrel, so that when drawn out and moved to one side the rod could be pushed into the chambers of the cylinder. A gate in the recoil plate permitted cartridges to be loaded or ejected as in the Colt. Comparative dimensions of the pistols were as follows:

	Forehand & Wadsworth	Colt
Total length, inches	13.15	12.5
Length of barrel, inches	7.5	7.5
Diameter of bore, inches	0.435	0.45
Grooves, depth, inches	0.0075	0.005
Grooves, number of	6	6
Twist uniform, one turn in inches	2.88	16
Weight, pounds	2.31	2.31

Only minor differences having to do with the locking of the ejector rod existed between the two Forehand & Wadsworth revolvers. The board noted that their ejector mechanism had a "neat and attractive" appearance but criticized its frailty, as well as the close fit between the cylinder and frame and the freedom of the former to revolve backwards or forwards at half cock, obstructing entry of the ejector rod. In loading, firing and ejecting tests conducted with standard service ammunition of .45 calibre, the Colt performed with substantially greater rapidity and without misfires that in the Forehand & Wadsworth were attributed to a failure to index properly. There was no material difference between the pistols in deviation or penetration.

It was, however, in the rust test that the Forehand & Wadsworth fared worst. After twenty-four hours rusting its ejector rod could not be drawn out without a vise, the cylinder stop would not function, and there was difficulty in closing the loading gate. In firing it worked "with considerable difficulty," while the working qualities of the Colt were unimpaired. After forty-eight hours the Forehand & Wadsworth cocked and uncocked with such difficulty that it "could scarcely be worked," whereas the Colt functioned without difficulty once a couple of shots had been fired. The conclusions of the board were as follows:

> The material points of difference between the Forehand & Wadsworth pistol and the Colts pistol, are decidedly in favor of the latter. The ungainly appearance of the ejecting rod of the Colt pistol is sought to be improved, in the Forehand & Wadsworth, at the expense of other and more important considerations . . . to eject a single shell requires seven distinct motions, while one motion in the Colt model accomplishes the same end . . . the delicacy of the ejecting rod . . . its compactness and general symmetry while recommending it for private personal use (where frequent ejection of shells is not required) . . . are fatal to this weapon for service. . . . Other defective conditions . . . are not so much in *kind* as in *degree:* feeble springs . . . shallow stop notches . . . backward rotary motion of the cylinder . . . defective working of the breech gate . . . no safety notch. . . .

The date of the trial makes it apparent that the specimens examined were of the first model of single action army revolver marked on the barrel "FOREHAND & WADSWORTH, WORCESTER, MASS. U. S. PAT'D OCT 22 '61. JUNE 27 '71 OCT 28 '73." It is noteworthy that these patents all covered features meeting with criticism from the ordnance board. The first, issued to Ethan Allen (#33,509), related to the action of the cylinder stop which the report characterized as "weak." The second (#116,522) taken by Sullivan Forehand and Henry C. Wadsworth, covered the housing of the ejector rod inside the removable cylinder pin. This feature was the principal novelty of the Forehand & Wadsworth though not one that commended itself to the ordnance board. Jacob Rupertus of Philadelphia was the last patentee, and evidently assigned this reissue (#5631) of his earlier patent of July 19, 1864.

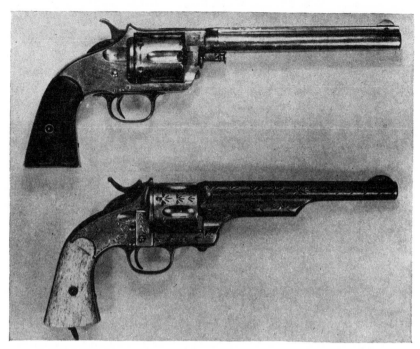

Forehand & Wadsworth and Merwin Hulbert Army Revolvers
Courtesy of James E. Serven

Its relevant portion covered the hinged loading gate of the breech plate, which the board found would not always close tightly. A fourth patent already held by Forehand and Wadsworth covered a brake which would have obviated the criticized free turning of the cylinder at half cock. Ironically enough, it was not incorporated in the design of the army model. None of this model was purchased by the Ordnance Department, although a number in .44 calibre centerfire were sold to the public. The design was altered about 1878 and the frail ejector rod replaced by a side ejector.

Apart from alterations developed by the Ordnance Department itself, the last single action rival of the Peacemaker to be tested was a revolver submitted by Merwin, Hulbert & Co. of previous mention. A board consisting of Captain George

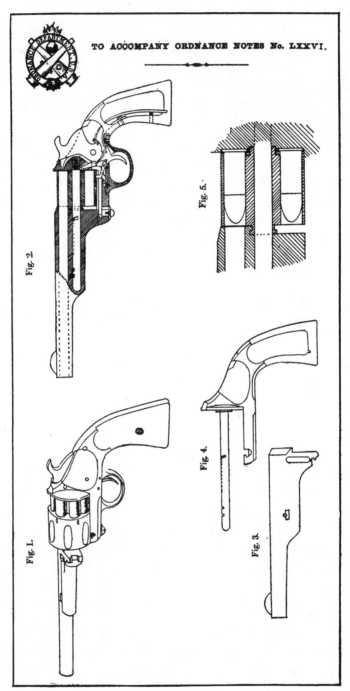

Fig. 2.

Fig. 5.

Fig. 1.

Fig. 4.

Fig. 3.

Diagrams of Merwin Hulbert Army Revolver

W. McKee and Lieutenant John E. Greer reported on it at the Springfield Armory. Tests similar to the earlier ones of 1876 were applied to this pistol, the results being recorded in Ordnance Notes, No. LXXVI dated January 22, 1878. The Merwin Hulbert loaded through a gate like the Colt, and its lock mechanism resembled the Schofield. Its peculiar features were an open top and a cylinder and barrel which when unlocked from the frame could be rotated to the left and slid forward on the base pin. This would draw from the chambers the cartridges whose heads were retained by an extractor ring on the recoil plate. Diagrams of the arm are reproduced here, as is a table of dimensions and weights. In a test of initial velocity, a mean of 656', one foot per second better than the Remington Model of 1875, was found, and penetration and recoil were recorded at 45 and 74 respectively, as compared to 43 and 53 for the Remington. Figures for the latter are cited because both were tested with a .44 calibre cartridge rather than the service .45. The time re-

---

MERWIN HULBERT

DIMENSIONS:

Total length, inches	12.50
Length of barrel, inches	7
Diameter of bore, inches	0.42
Grooves, width of, inches	0.12
Grooves, depth of, inches	0.005
Grooves, uniform twist of, one turn in inches . .	21.43
Grooves, number of	5
Chambers, number of	6
Chambers, diameter of, inches	0.44
Cylinder, length of, inches	1.50
Cylinder, diameter of, inches	1.735

WEIGHTS:

Total weight	2 lbs., 11¼ oz.
Weight of powder, grains	23
Weight of bullet, grains	252

quired to dismount the revolver completely was 8 minutes 15 seconds and for assembly 14 minutes, longer in the first case and shorter in the second than for any of the other pistols. Rapidity of loading for 18 shots and ejecting was 1 minute, 45 seconds, slightly better than the Colt. Other tests may be quoted verbatim:

ENDURANCE

Two hundred and fifty rounds were fired, the revolver working without difficulty throughout. It was allowed five minutes to cool after each 50 rounds.

FOULING

The revolver remained uncleaned forty-eight hours, after which it was fired 50 rounds. It was allowed five minutes to cool after the 12th, 24th, and 36th rounds. Though badly fouled at the rear of the cylinder, by the escape of gas at the primer (the ammunition being outside priming), the arm worked satisfactorily.

DUSTING TEST

The revolver was next cleaned and thoroughly dusted with fine sand. It was then wiped off with the hands alone. Twelve rounds were fired. The revolver was then dusted as before, to ascertain the combined effects of dusting and fouling. Six rounds were fired. The revolver worked freely throughout.

The usual rusting tests with sal ammoniac were applied, after the second of which the hammer and trigger required scraping in order to function. The base pin was so rusted that the barrel had to be held in a vise "in order to complete the turning and draw it to the front along the pin." Noting that it required twenty minutes to restore the pistol to firing condition, the board remarked that "considering how badly the pistol was rusted, it worked very satisfactorily." In conclusion, the board found:

The objectionable features as compared with the Colt are: Its greater weight (about 5 ounces); its less favorable balance in the barrel, owing to its center of gravity being well forward; its single surface of rotation for the cylinder; its greater number of parts (about 20), and the fact there are many sizes of screws, necessitating the use of several screwdrivers. . . . Finally the whole system is not a rigid one, as in the Colt. The barrel is placed on a base pin and is locked to the lower portion of the frame. More or less motion can and does take place around the pin, which will be increased as the base-pin and locking device wear away. Its advantages as compared with the Colt are: Its neater appearance, and its dispensing with the outside ejecting mechanism, which frequently becomes disabled by the breaking off of the ejector-head. Occasionally the ejecting tube itself is carried away. The form of the recoil-plate and the extractor-ring, preventing as they do sand, etc., from clogging the working of the cylinder, must also be considered as advantageous.

On the whole, the Board regards this as a very good pistol, it having endured the tests in a fairly satisfactory manner.

Such praise was too faint to induce the Government to purchase any of the Merwin Hulberts, which sold commercially, however, in substantial quantities. Merwin, Hulbert & Co., successors of Merwin & Bray, were dealers in firearms at 245 Broadway, New York City. They were not themselves manufacturers, the pistols bearing their name being made for them by Hopkins & Allen, of Norwich, Connecticut, as markings indicate. The open top design of the Merwin Hulbert, somewhat of an anomaly after the advent of the cartridge revolver, was based on two patents taken March 6, 1877. One (#187,980) by Daniel Moore, an inventor whose name is often associated with cartridge deringers, covered a barrel and cylinder which could be rotated to move forward on a center pin slotted diagonally and longitudinally. The other by William A. Hulbert (#187,975) covered a flange on the outside of the recoil plate to hold the cartridge heads in the

fixed annular extractor. Both these patents were refinements
of earlier ones granted December 15, 1874, to Moore and
April 21, 1874, to Benjamin H. Williams. The latter was the
initial patent on an extractor ring affixed to the standing
breech, and entering a recess in the base of the cylinder.

The Merwin Hulbert provided a third distinct design of
military revolver beside the solid frame, ejector rod models
of Colt, Remington and Forehand & Wadsworth and the top
break, lifting extractor system of Smith & Wesson. Its great

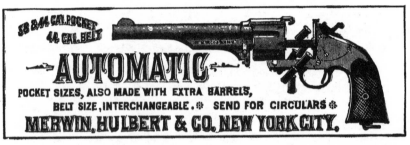

Advertisement from the *Army and Navy Journal*, 1882

virtue, apart from a streamlined silhouette, was the screw action by which the barrel and cylinder could be started forward along the center pin, away from exploded cartridges
held by the fixed extractor ring. In the days of imperfect cases
that were prone to stick in the chamber this was an important feature, but one that lost significance with the perfec-
tion of centerfire cartridge design. The Merwin Hulbert had
a strong enough frame, and was well fabricated, but very
likely because of the passing need for so powerful an extractor
system it did not stand the test of time. Double actions in
various calibres were made and a top strap added to the
single action, which was extensively advertised under the
caption "Automatic" in the *Army and Navy Journal* of 1882.[2]
About 1886 manufacture of the .44 calibre Merwin Hulbert
was discontinued.

VIII

ADOPTION
OF THE DOUBLE ACTION

THE single action .45 calibre Colt continued to be purchased by the Ordnance Department in orders of several thousand a year long after the development of double action weapons by Colt's and other manufacturers. Yet the newer models did not escape the attention of ordnance officers. Captain O. E. Michaelis of previous mention, to whom a new double action .45 Colt was presented in June, 1878, by General William B. Franklin, Vice-President of Colt's, wrote from the Department of Dakota:

> All who have seen it pronounce it the best revolver yet made. It is well-balanced and well-proportioned. I have asked for 100 to be issued to Cav'y companies for trials. The Colts has been made the weapon of the 7th Cav'y by a regimental order.

Colonel Benton of the Springfield Armory, noting Michaelis' request, wrote to General Franklin August 5, 1878:

> I have never seen one of these arms and would be glad to have the loan of one for examination. What do you think of them for military purposes?

In forwarding General Franklin's reply to the Chief of Ordnance, Colonel Benton noted: [1]

> The only advantage that this system possesses is, that the arm can be fired rapidly without disturbing the aim. The disadvantages are, liability to accidental discharge, and failure to explode

73

VOLUME XVI.—NUMBER 4. } WHOLE NUMBER 784. }

NEW YORK, SATURDAY, AUGUST 31, 1878.

{ SIX DOLLARS PER YEAR. { SINGLE COPIES, FIFTEEN CENTS

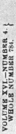
From the *Army and Navy Journal*

the cartridge. The reason for the first will be apparent to any one who examines the arm. While experimenting with one of the two pistols sent to this Armory by Gen[1] Franklin one of them was fired prematurely, although the person handling it was careful and experienced. He is unable to state the precise cause of the accident.

Out of 100 trials of one of these arms there were seven misfires. The liability to misfire arises from the necessity of making the mainspring so weak that its pressure may be overcome by the finger pulling on the trigger.

This unfavorable comment appears to have foreclosed further interest on the part of the Ordnance Department in the new double action .45. While another specimen was sent to the Springfield Arsenal in October, 1879, Government purchases did not follow. The arm was popular, however, with Army officers, who bought it privately.

In 1887 the Ordnance Department experimented with a "safety stop" for the single action "by which the accidental discharge of the cocked revolver in ranks will be prevented." This was one of a series of devices invented by Colonel John C. Kelton, Assistant Adjutant General, U. S. A. It consisted of a thumb-operated safety pin which—unless disengaged—arrested movement of the hammer at full cock.[2] Colonel Kelton's patent specification declared that "with mounted men using the pistol in hand-to-hand conflict there is always danger to comrades in the ranks by the premature discharge of weapons, either on account of the unmanageableness of the horses or from convulsive movement of a man who has himself been shot." The drawings show the device adapted to a Schofield revolver, but according to the patent it could "be applied by various methods to different pistols." Twenty-five Schofield revolvers were fitted by the Ordnance Department with Colonel Kelton's safety stop and issued to Captain C. C. C. Carr, First Cavalry, for trial at Fort Leavenworth.

In the same year as this Army experiment the Navy Ordnance Bureau began to test a new model of Colt, a six shot .38 calibre double action, with solid frame and cylinder swinging sideways to permit simultaneous ejection. At that time the stock of revolvers which the Navy had on hand were obsolete weapons which the Chief of the Bureau described as having "come down from the war." [3] Many of these were converted 1851 Navy revolvers which had been sent to the Colt factory for alteration to .38 centerfire in 1873. Following adoption by the Navy of the new Colt .38, for which an initial order of 5,000 was placed in 1888,[4] a trial was conducted at the Springfield Armory of this pistol and a .38 calibre five shot double action safety hammerless Smith & Wesson. The same tests as had been standardized for revolvers in 1876 were applied by the board which consisted of Captain J. C. Clifford and Lieutenant J. W. Benét. Its conclusions were: [5]

that the Smith & Wesson revolver has passed all the tests satisfactorily except the rust test, in which it was totally disabled. The Colt revolver has passed all the tests satisfactorily except the dust test, in which it was disabled as a double-action revolver, but could be worked satisfactorily by cocking the hammer as in a single-action revolver. Whether these arms have the necessary stopping power the Board has no means of determining. The Board is of the opinion that the issue of a limited number of each of these arms would be advantageous as affording a comparison between the double-acting system and the single-action system in use in the service. Each of the revolvers possesses advantages peculiar to itself, and a competitive test in service would be necessary to determine definitely which is the superior.

On April 5, 1890, the *Army and Navy Journal* made note of an endorsement by Colonel Elmer Otis, Eighth Cavalry, "reporting the result of the past year's experience with the Colt revolver [.45 calibre], proving beyond question that it is an inferior weapon from several causes." The nature of the

defects was not disclosed in this comment, but they seem to
have had to do with two functions peculiar to the single action
—rod ejection and hand cocking. A contemporary writer in
The Cavalry Journal [6] found a tendency in the ejector spring
to become weak so that when the arm was raised for cocking
the rod would fall into a chamber and prevent rotation. The
same article asserted that sticking of cartridge shells not in-

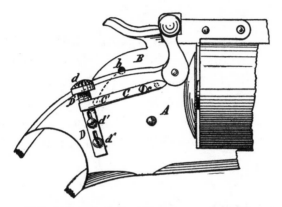

Col. Kelton's Safety Stop, patented 1885

frequently disabled the Government issue Colt, although
those purchased from private firms gave no trouble. Possible
variation in arsenal-loaded shells was not mentioned. The author observed that "our pistols have not had much use of late
years; and, though often carried, have principally been worn
out in the holster."

Other officers noted the problems involved in cocking the
single action for rapid fire. Captain William Preble Hall of
the Fifth Cavalry wrote: [7] "The difficulty in cocking the revolver is added to considerably when the horse is in rapid motion. Our Colt's revolver is as much inferior to some of the
double action ones, as the old muzzle to the modern breech
loader." He went on to say: "The calibre .45 Smith & Wesson,
is, if anything, a more indifferent weapon than the Colt's."

Lieutenant H. L. Ripley of the Third Cavalry wrote to Colt's on March 6, 1890:

The Army Colt about which I wrote . . . is all right except when cocking it at a full gallop by throwing it forward quickly from the vertical position of "raise" as recommended by the tactics. It is thrown forward with a jerk cocking it at the same time and the trouble is that it revolves too far or not far enough, usually the former, so that when pulled the hammer does not strike on the centre of the cartridge.

The writer went on to say that having tried several pistols with the same result, he believed that the defect in indexing was inherent in the single action, but that it would be obviated in a self-cocking pistol.

Inquiry by the aforementioned Colonel Otis as to whether the Smith & Wesson double action revolver could be obtained was made the occasion for an official statement which the Chief of Ordnance was careful to say had the approval of the Commanding General of the Army: [8]

The amount of funds available is not sufficient to permit filling requisitions for Smith & Wesson double action revolvers. It is also deemed unwise to issue an untried arm in large quantities before a preliminary field test has demonstrated its serviceability. This department has already made arrangements to issue one hundred each of the .38 calibre double action Colt's new navy revolvers with improved ejector and a .38 calibre double action safety hammerless Smith & Wesson revolver with 250 rounds of ammunition per revolver for competitive field trials. These arms will be ready for issue in about three months.

The Report of the Chief of Ordnance for 1891 stated that the revolvers "have been on trial with nine troops of the First, Third, Fifth, Sixth, Eighth and Ninth Cavalry. The reports which have been received from the troop commanders with two exceptions favor the Colt revolver and consider it a very decided improvement upon the calibre .45 Colt now in service." [9] The service trial was followed by another at the Springfield Armory conducted by a board consisting of Captain S. E. Blount and Lieutenant F. P. Peck. Their report revealed that of thirteen cavalry officers to whom the revolvers had been submitted, eleven expressed an unqualified preference for the .38 Colt, one for the Smith & Wesson, [10] and one, while favoring the .38 Colt over the Smith & Wesson, preferred to either of them "the present .45 Calibre Colt on account of its heavier bullet, and consequent greater stopping power." [11] After concurring in the general preference for the .38 Colt over the Smith & Wesson, the board stated: [12]

Between the .38 caliber Colt and the .45 caliber Colt now in service the preference, in the opinion of the board, should be awarded to the former, on account, principally, of its less weight and size, its greater ease and rapidity of ejecting and loading, its greater accuracy, and, above all, its adaptability for use as either a single or double action revolver, and its full equality with the present service arm in all other essential features.

To the latter statement but one exception can be advanced—its diminished "stopping power" as compared with the larger revolver. That the stopping power is less is of course evident, but that is no material disadvantage if it still remains sufficient. The question can only be definitely settled by actual trial against living objects, and until the revolver is tested in action the opinions of the cavalry officers who have used the weapons afford the best available evidence.

The board then went on to recommend that if the .38 Colt were adopted, it should be modified by strengthening the rebound spring of the trigger and the locking device of the cylinder. In the latter respect the first model relied only on the rotating hand, but notches in the periphery of the cylinder and a lock and stop engaging them except when the trigger was in motion were subsequently added. On April 19, 1892, the Chief of Ordnance, Brigadier General D. W. Flagler, recommended to the Secretary of War, whose approval was given April 25,[13]

the adoption of .38 caliber for the military service revolver, in place of .45 caliber, as now prescribed. This recommendation is based upon the favorable outcome of trials of .38 caliber revolvers which have been made during the past two years. After trial by

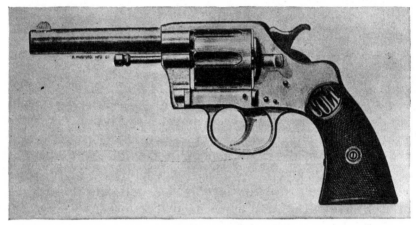

Colt's Double Action .38, from *Franklin Institute Journal,* 1890

a board of officers at the Springfield Armory, in 1889, two hundred of .38 caliber revolvers were procured and issued to troops in the field, where they were subjected to a crucial test. Certain minor defects only were developed. The reports of the company commander who tested the arms in the field, and a revolver with the minor defects corrected, were some months ago submitted to another board at the Springfield Armory, and the arm is now perfected and ready for service. The subject of the best caliber to adopt in connection with modern changes in small arms and the best results obtained in other countries in connection with the peculiar ballistic properties required for a revolver has during these years received careful study, and many experiments have been made. The results indicate and prove that the caliber .38 is the best for us to adopt.

Five thousand was the initial order placed with Colt's Patent Fire Arms Manufacturing Company, and these revolvers were issued during the year 1893.[14] Doubts as to stopping power expressed by the officers previously mentioned were shared by one of the world's greatest authorities on small

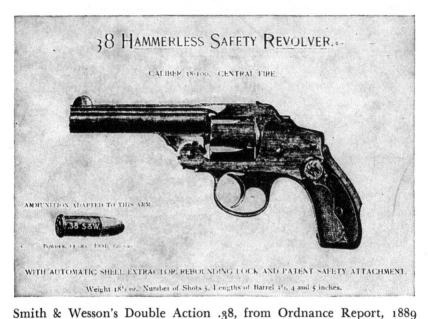

Smith & Wesson's Double Action .38, from Ordnance Report, 1889

arms, Lieutenant Colonel G. W. Fosbery, V.C., late of the Bengal Staff Corps. In a London lecture to members of the Royal United Service Institution he observed in 1896 regarding modern revolvers: [15]

While almost every pistol is made sufficiently accurate to shoot well at distances at which it would be folly to use it, *stopping power* is, I fear, sadly neglected in almost all with which I am acquainted, whether Belgian, English or American, always excepting the Colt's Frontier Pistol carrying the cartridge of the Winchester Repeater. As, however, if only the bore is large enough, this power can be conferred by the use of a properly constructed bullet, and a charge of powder calculated rather for this purpose than for range and penetration, the fault can be remedied.

Colonel Fosbery knew what he was talking about from combat experience in India, where he won the British Empire's highest award for valor in action against Hindustani fanatics at the Umbeyla Pass in 1863.[16] He went on to say:

With the civilized man, who knows to a nicety the locality of his principal organs and something of the effects that the presence of foreign bodies in his interior may be expected to produce, a comparatively slight wound (surgically considered) will often suffice to set him thinking of his spiritual condition or his other personal interests, rather than of the business in which he may be engaged. Thus, a comparatively feeble weapon may often be used against him with good effect. But when we are fighting the Ghasi, the Zulu, or the Arab of the Soudan, the case is very different. Any one of these will make his rush, having his mind fully made up to kill you, or to be killed by you, and one of these two things he will get done without *arrière-pensée* of any kind, and he knows as little about his own inside as a tiger does. As in the case of that beast also, when he makes his attack upon you a personal one, you must be prepared to stop him or die.

It was not until the Philippine Insurrection that "actual trial against living objects" demonstrated that the 150 grain bullet of the .38 calibre Colt was inadequate to stop the Moro juramentadoes, and the United States Army went back to the .45. Major (later General) Robert Lee Bullard, a veteran of the Philippine fighting, has described the situation graphically: [17]

No better test of our revolver's worth and the fitness of its caliber for the purpose for which a revolver has been provided can be had or ever has been had than in its recent use by our troops fighting in the Moro country. When they fight, Moros fight suddenly at close quarters in the revolver's domain of twenty paces. It is a damning comment on the caliber of the .38 that every officer, man and camp-follower in the regiments which have served against Moros after a first experience laid aside the .38 whenever he could by hook or crook raise a bigger "gun," generally the old .45. Indeed a department commander, who by constant personal part with troops in the field knew the need, provided and issued to officers and men as many as he could get of .45 revolvers, gladly taking even the old style, slow-working, single-action ones.

Major Bullard's comment clarifies the common belief that the gun utilized against the Moros was the so-called "Alaskan Model" of the double action .45 Colt revolver, distinguished by its extra size trigger and guard designed to permit firing with gloves on. Colt's old shipping ledgers indicate that about 4,600 of these with six inch barrels were delivered to the Springfield Armory between April and December, 1902, the serial numbers running from 43,401 to 48,097. Yet as has already been mentioned the factory had in the previous year shipped a quantity of refinished Army single action .45s direct to Manila. Thus the Peacemaker played a part too in stopping "living objects."

IX

POPULARITY
OF THE MODEL "P"

ORIGIN of the trade name Peacemaker for the Colt .45 is somewhat obscure. It was employed by B. Kittredge & Co. and other agents of Colt's in their first advertisements of the arm, yet it is pure coincidence that all pistols made on the large single action solid frame are today known at the Colt factory as Model "P." When the single action was chambered in 1878 for the .44-40 cartridge of the Winchester rifle, it was advertised and marked "Frontier Six Shooter." [1] The name Peacemaker was only applied to the revolver in .45 calibre, and by the 1880s this model was more commonly known and called the "Single Action Army." Its baptismal name apparently derives from a nickname for Samuel Colt, who as early as April 1, 1847, was jocularly addressed as "Peace maker" by Captain Samuel H. Walker. [2] Popular terms for the Peacemaker, which itself became a colloquialism, were "thumb-buster," "plowhandle," "hog leg," "equalizer" or "forty-five." All these primarily connoted the single action Colt, while other slang such as "six-gun" or "shooting iron" meant a revolver in the more generic sense. [3]

As has been mentioned already, the Model "P" pistol has had the longest period of popularity of any sort of revolver in the world. Starting in 1873, it remained continuously in production until 1941, when the machinery used to make it was displaced to permit machine gun manufacture for World

84

War II. This suspension is still continuing, and a letter from the President of Colt's Manufacturing Company in the April, 1949, issue of *The American Rifleman* indicates that it will be permanent. This decision having been based on factors of supply and demand, it could be reversed by the same process.

The highest extant serial number for the Model "P," which, with a single exception hereafter noted, includes every

Presentation to Buffalo Bill by a member of his Wild West Show
Courtesy of Gerald Fox

type and calibre made on the large single action solid frame, is at the present writing 357,859. This is a fair indication of the volume of production over sixty-eight years, and it exceeds the record for any other kind of single action revolver, whether of Colt or other make, and including percussion arms. An impression of the great vogue of the Model "P" over the course of time may be gained from the following table of annual production, which is approximate only, having been compiled from old shipping records available for specific verification to police authorities only. Note should be particularly taken that the margin of error in serial numbers may be as great as a year in either direction and that not every frame stamped with a number passed final factory inspection. The indications are that an average of about ⅓ of 1% was rejected for defects and scrapped.

MODEL "P"

Year	Serial Range	Annual Production
1873	1 to 200	200
1874	201 to 15,000	14,800
1875	15,001 to 22,000	7,000
1876	22,001 to 33,000	11,000
1877	33,001 to 41,000	8,000
1878	41,001 to 49,000	8,000
1879	49,001 to 53,000	4,000
1880	53,001 to 62,000	9,000
1881	62,001 to 73,000	11,000
1882	73,001 to 85,000	12,000
1883	85,001 to 102,000	17,000
1884	102,001 to 114,000	12,000
1885	114,001 to 117,000	3,000
1886	117,001 to 119,000	2,000
1887	119,001 to 125,000	6,000
1888	125,001 to 128,000	3,000
1889	128,001 to 130,000	2,000
1890	130,001 to 136,000	6,000
1891	136,001 to 144,000	8,000
1892	144,001 to 149,000	5,000
1893	149,001 to 154,000	5,000
1894	154,001 to 159,000	5,000
1895	159,001 to 163,000	4,000
1896	163,001 to 168,000	5,000
1897	168,001 to 175,000	7,000
1898	175,001 to 182,000	7,000
1899	182,001 to 192,000	10,000
1900	192,001 to 203,000	11,000
1901	203,001 to 220,000	17,000
1902	220,001 to 238,000	18,000
1903	238,001 to 250,000	12,000
1904	250,001 to 261,000	11,000
1905	261,001 to 273,000	12,000
1906	273,001 to 288,000	15,000

MODEL "P"

Year	Serial Range	Annual Production
1907	288,001 to 304,000	16,000
1908	304,001 to 308,000	4,000
1909	308,001 to 312,000	4,000
1910	312,001 to 316,000	4,000
1911	316,001 to 321,000	5,000
1912	321,001 to 325,000	4,000
1913	325,001 to 328,000	3,000
1914	328,001 to 329,500	1,500
1915	329,501 to 332,000	2,500
1916	332,001 to 335,000	3,000
1917	335,001 to 337,000	2,000
1918	337,001 to 337,200	200
1919	337,201 to 338,000	800
1920	338,001 to 341,000	3,000
1921	341,001 to 343,000	2,000
1922	343,001 to 344,500	1,500
1923	344,501 to 346,400	1,900
1924	346,401 to 347,300	900
1925	347,301 to 348,200	900
1926	348,201 to 349,800	1,600
1927	349,801 to 351,300	1,500
1928	351,301 to 352,400	1,100
1929	352,401 to 353,800	1,400
1930	353,801 to 354,100	400
1931	354,101 to 354,500	400
1932	354,501 to 354,800	300
1933	354,801 to 355,000	200
1934	355,001 to 355,200	200
1935	355,201 to 355,300	100
1936	355,301 to 355,400	100
1937	355,401 to 356,100	700
1938	356,101 to 356,600	500
1939	356,601 to 357,000	400
1940	357,001 to 357,859	859

The impact of war and depression in the foregoing table is marked, not only for the immediate period but in the demand that came after. Thus, although the Peacemaker was no longer an official military weapon at the time of the Spanish-American War, one finds production stimulated in 1897 and 1898, but not reaching a peak until later. History repeated itself on a lesser scale in the period of World War I. The great depression of the 1930s is likewise charted quite accurately in these figures. But perhaps most significant of all are the two production pinnacles of the early 1880s and of 1899 to 1907. The first coincided with the climax of the struggles between rancher and rustler, marshal and outlaw, cattleman and nester, in the frontier communities of the West.[4] The second reflected a renewed demand for the sturdy single action in the mining camps of the Klondike and on both sides of the Mexican Border. Range wars between cattlemen and sheepmen likewise extended into this period.

Much romantic literature ranging from Owen Wister's *The Virginian* to the latest exploit of the Lone Ranger has been written around the six-shooter, and it remains today the standard firearm of the Hollywood "horse opera" or "oater." In all this folklore there is seldom any pistol but a Colt single action in the hands of good men or bad. While anachronisms are often apparent where the setting is prior to 1874, the most common one being the portrayal of a Peacemaker in the hands of veterans returning from the War Between the States, preferential exemplification of the Colt is historically quite valid.

Apart from the volume of the contemporary demand, an impression of the appeal which the Peacemaker had may be gained from the nature of the early orders placed for it. Like other models, it was sold by Colt's mainly through wholesalers, but the Company permitted officers and men of the United States forces to purchase direct at a discount, and extended a similar privilege to sheriffs and other peace officers. Likewise, individual orders for specially finished arms appear to have been filled direct. Beginning in the late 1870s, the Peacemaker was not infrequently supplied with engraved parts plated in nickel, silver or gold, and with German silver front sights, either of the half moon or bead variety. Handles of oak, maple, ebony, rosewood or sycamore, or of buffalo horn, ivory or mother of pearl were furnished on special order. The latter were often etched or carved, usual designs being a steer, ox or buffalo head, or an American or Mexican eagle. Occasionally the carving was of the head of a horse, bull or ram, or a bunch of grapes. An order of 1879 is on record for a carved pearl handle having a "Texas steer" on one side and "the goddess of love" on the other. This motif had variations—an ox head and a woman and serpent being one, a bull head and the goddess of liberty or justice another. A third design substituted a nude woman for deity, balanced by a bird dog or a five pointed star. Emblems were sometimes combined with initials, one ingenious example having a steer branded DH carved on one grip with the monogram DWH on the other. The decoration of handles occasionally took the form of inset coins or Masonic symbols.

Inscriptions were likewise engraved or inlaid on the backstraps of presentation arms by special order. The first Peacemakers recorded as so marked were a lot of six .45s with 7½ inch barrels, ivory handles and nickel-plated engraved finish. They left the factory in July, 1878, with the following names inscribed on the backstraps: P. T. Swaine, D. D. Mitchell, S. R. Stafford, G. K. McGunnegle, J. F. Hegewald and B. N. Waters. These gentlemen were all officers of the 15th Infantry Regiment, United States Army, then stationed at Fort Wingate, New Mexico.[5] Lieutenant Colonel Peter Tyler Swaine, a West Pointer, had been colonel of an Ohio regiment during

COLT'S PATENT FIRE ARMS MANUFACTURING COMPANY, HARTFORD, CONN. U. S. A.

NEW MODEL ARMY METALLIC CARTRIDGE REVOLVING PISTOL.

The Drawing is one-half size of the Pistol.

Price, $16.00.

It has been adopted by the War Department for the Cavalry Service of the United States.

The length of the Pistol is 12½ inches; length of barrel, 7½ inches; its bore or calibre, .45 inch. Weight, 2 lbs., 5 oz. Rifling, six grooves, one revolution in 16 inches; depth of groove, .005 inch. Number of chambers in cylinder, six.

Length of barrel 4¾, 5½, and 7½ inches, with ejectors.   Length of barrel 3½, and 4 inches, without ejectors.
Cartridge, .45 inch calibre; weight of powder, 30 grains; weight of lead, 250 grains. Central fire, external priming.
We can also furnish this arm to use the .44 Russian, .44 calibre long and short, .38 calibre long and short, .32 and .22 calibre cartridges.

IT DIFFERS FROM OTHER REVOLVING PISTOLS IN THE FOLLOWING POINTS, VIZ.:

The hand, or finger, or pawl, which revolves the cylinder, has two points, one above the other. The upper engages the ratchet of the cylinder when the revolution begins, but before the necessary kick of a revolution could be made, as the pawl moves in a plane, and the ratchet tooth in the arc of a circle whose plane is perpendicular to the pawl's plane of motion, the pawl would lose its hold on the tooth, and the revolution of the cylinder would stop. To prevent this, the second point is added, and just as the first point will disengage from the ratchet, the second, another tooth of the ratchet gives complete, and therefore this arrangement the pawl actuates a larger ratchet than it could otherwise, and therefore exerts more force upon the cylinder, by acting upon a longer lever-arm. This permits a smaller sized cylinder for the same diameter of ratchet.

The cylinder has a bushing, which projects in front of it, and gives three surfaces upon which the cylinder revolves, thus diminishing the chance of sticking from dirt or rust, and also giving a very small axis upon which to revolve, decreasing the moment of friction.

When the ejector is used a spring runs back to its place and is ready for use again, avoiding the necessity of putting it back.

To TAKE APART THE PISTOL.—Half-cock the pistol, loosen the catch-screw which holds the centre-pin, draw out the centre-pin, open the gate, and the cylinder can then be withdrawn.

To remove the ejector, turn out the ejector tube-screw, then push the front end away from the barrel and pull it towards the muzzle. The barrel can then be unscrewed.

The stock can be removed by turning out the two screws just behind the hammer, and that at the bottom of the strap. All the parts of the lock are then displayed, and can be readily separated.

The cylinder-bushing should be pushed out for cleaning.

To remove the gate, turn out a screw in the lower side of the frame, (hidden by the trigger guard,) then the gate-spring and catch can be withdrawn, and the gate can be pushed out. The best sperm oil should be used for oiling the parts.

To LOAD THE PISTOL.—1st motion: holding the pistol in the left hand, muzzle downwards, and with the right hand half-cock, and open the gate. 2d motion: insert the cartridges in succession, with the right forefinger and the right hand, and fire it, (taking it in the right hand,) or bring the hammer to the safety notch as may be desired.

To EJECT THE CARTRIDGE SHELLS.—1st motion: holding the pistol in the left hand, half-cock with the right hand and open the gate. 2d motion: eject the shells in succession with the right hand, by use of the ejector, with the thumb or fore-finger of the left hand. When the shells have been ejected, the pistol is ready for the 2d motion of loading.

N. B.—There are three notches in the hammer of this pistol. The first is the safety-notch, the second is the half-cock notch, and the third is the cock-notch. The pistol cannot be fired when the hammer rests in the safety-notch or half-cock notch, and can be fired by putting the trigger when the hammer rests in the cock-notch. The pistol should be carried habitually with the hammer resting in the safety-notch.

"THE FRONTIER."—This most popular Revolving Pistol is the same as that described above, and is designed to fill the want of a Revolving Pistol using the same ammunition as a magazine rifle and thus avoid the necessity of carrying two kinds of ammunition, besides the many other apparent advantages which make this arm a necessity to the practical sportsman and frontiersman.

"THE FRONTIER" is made to use the .32-100, .38-100, and .44-100 Colt's Lightning Magazine Rifle Cartridges and also those of same calibre used in other magazine and single shot rifles. All of above revolvers can be furnished with case hardened frame and blued barrel or nickel plated and with wood or rubber stocks as desired, at same prices. All barrels over 7½ inches long, $1.00 extra per each additional inch.

From Colt's first full length Catalog, 1888

the War of 1861-1865. First Lieutenant Stephen Randall Stafford, another veteran of the War in which he was brevetted a major, was regimental quartermaster. George Kennedy McGunnegle was a first lieutenant of Company D, and David Dawson Mitchell, John Frederick Charles Hegewald and Basil Norris Waters were second lieutenants. The 15th Infantry campaigned against the Apaches and later in the Philippines, where Mitchell, then a captain, was killed in action at Mavitac on September 17, 1900. The occasion for this joint order of revolvers is not known, but the Peacemaker was currently being advertised in the *Army and Navy Journal*,[6] where the officers might have seen it while on headquarters duty at Fort Wingate during the winter of 1877.

The next inscribed Peacemaker, a silver-plated arm with 7½ inch barrel and pearl handles carved with a Mexican eagle, shipped in October, 1879, was recorded as having been marked "W. B. Masterson." William Barclay Masterson, better known as Bat, was sheriff of Ford County, Kansas. He had been one of the buffalo hunters who held off the Comanches at Adobe Walls in 1874, later hiring out as a scout for General Nelson A. Miles. In 1876 prior to becoming a proprietor of the Lone Star Dance Hall he served as a deputy of Wyatt Earp, Marshal of Dodge City.[7] Bat was evidently well pleased with the Peacemaker acquired by him while sheriff, for at different times subsequently he ordered seven more Colt single action forty-fives, either for himself or friends, the last two having "sights higher than usual."

Inscriptions on other Peacemakers are equally revealing of their clientele. "William R. Houston, Texas," was recorded for a presentation to a son of the victor at San Jacinto. "J. S. W. U.S.M. from the Boys, 1895" marked a gift to an unidentified federal marshal. "CB to BM 1886-1907" suggests a friendship or partnership of over twenty years' standing.

Dodge City, Kan.. July 24th 188 5

Colts F. A. Mfg Co

Hartford Conn
Gents

please send
me one of your Nickel plated short
45 Caliber Revolvers. it is for my
own use and for that reason I
would like to have a little Extra pains
taken with it. I am willing to pay
Extra for Extra work. Make it very
Easy on trigger and have the front
sight a little higher and thicker
than the ordinary pistol of this kind.
Put on a gutta percha handle and
send it as soon as possible.
have the barrel about the same length
that the Ejecting rod is.

28 B Express C. O. D.   Truly Yours
Mdse forward. Thursday July 30/85 ;   W. B. Masterson

P.S. Duplicate the above order by sending 2 —

Courtesy of Colt's Manufacturing Company

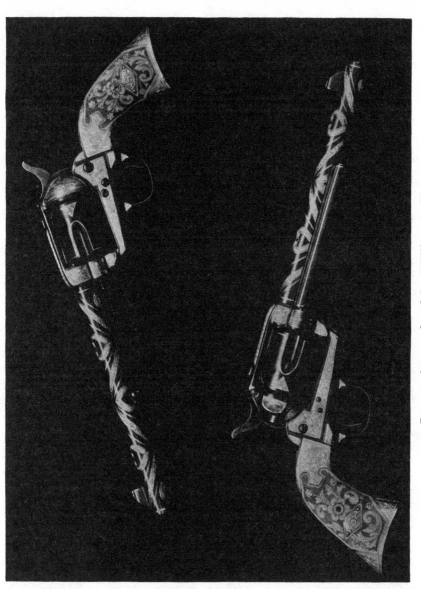

Peacemakers ordered by William S. Hart

Courtesy of Colt's Manufacturing Company

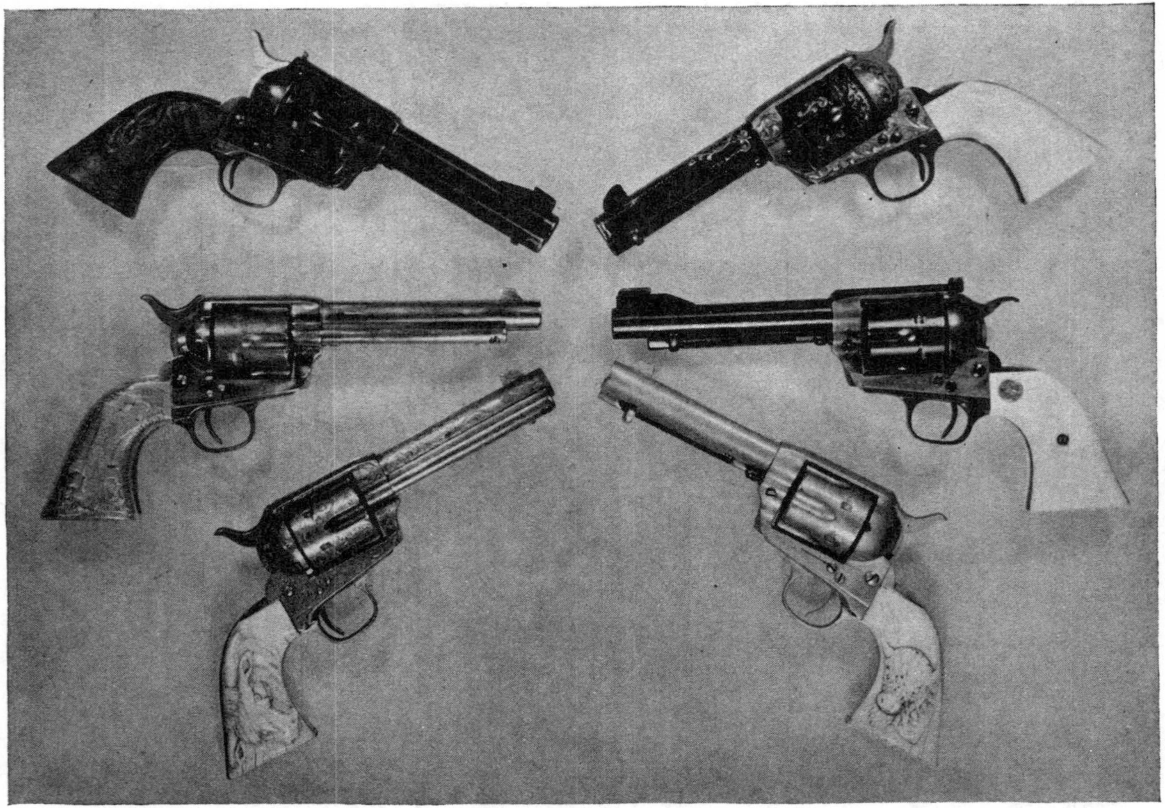

Courtesy of Roy S. Horton

"For our Chief W. M. Rea from Fort Worth Police" speaks for itself, as does "Robt. D. Weldrun from the Tomboy G. M. Co. Ltd. Telluride, Colo." "C. A. Farnsworth, Sheriff Grant Co. [N. M.] 1905-6" and "Paul Spofford Pearsall, Rough Rider USA" are equally self-explanatory. Fancy arms were often marked with addresses as well as names or initials, early examples being "Giles C. Avriet, Cameron Texas," "Ed Cornelius, Three Circle Ranch Erath Co.," "Jno. W. Parham, Hillsboro Texas," "Wm Reed, Antelope Springs, Col.," "Chas. Smith, Silver City N. M.," "O. W. Leader, Scipio, Okla." and "Wiley G. Hains, Hominy I.T." Hains was at the time chief of police for the Osage Nation and a deputy United States marshal. Names like those of two brothers, "Felipe Rodriguez" and "Tibucio Rodriguez" engraved on the pearl handles of pairs of silver-plated .44s exemplified the devotees of the single action south of the border.

Though not inscribed on the arms, names of other ultimate purchasers recorded in the 1890s have intriguing connotations, such as Departamento de Consignaciones, Soo Ho Sam, China-Japan Trading Co., Territorial Prison, Yuma, Harry Weir, Sect'y for Cowboy's Race, Copper Queen Consol. Mining Co., and Arizona Copper Co. In the early 1900s substantial purchases by the last two mentioned and Patagonia Mining Co., Alaska Juneau G. M. Co., Tiger Gold Co., Anaconda Copper Mining Co., Detroit Copper Mining Co. and Cananea Consol. Copper Co. of Sonora indicate that the Peacemaker had not lost its favor as a weapon for arming guards. Other large users often had the butts of their pistols marked with such legends as "Mex. Nat. R.R.," "W. F. & Co." [Wells-Fargo], "G. M. Parral" [Chihuahua mine], "E. de Mex." [Gov't of Mexico] and "S.A.P.D." [San Antonio Police Dept.]

Another feature of the Peacemaker supplied on special order was a barrel longer than the customary 7½ inches. An account of the presentation by Ned Buntline [8] of five such pieces having twelve inch barrels and detachable walnut rifle stocks is told in Stuart Lake's *Wyatt Earp, Frontier Marshal* (1931). These guns are reported to have been given by the originator of the dime novel to Wyatt Earp, Bat Masterson and other peace officers of Dodge City. Probably due to this

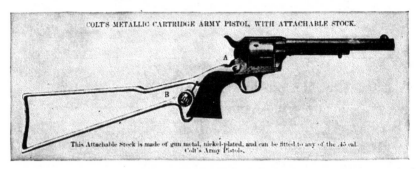

From Burr, *Four Thousand Years of World's Progress,* a report on the Philadelphia Centennial

account single actions fitted with shoulder stocks became known to collectors as "Buntline Specials." The making up of this special order has not been traced in the Colt Company's records, which do, however, indicate that Peacemakers with 10 inch and 16 inch barrels were supplied on occasion. B. Kittredge & Co. in December, 1877, ordered four 16 inchers, and in March, 1880, five more. Serial numbers of these pieces were in the same range as that of the specimen in the Ulrich Museum numbered 28809. This is equipped with a detachable skeleton shoulder stock, adjustable rear sight and front globe sight. Several 10 inch barrel Peacemakers equipped with peep and globe sights were also sold in 1878 and thereafter. Other odd barrel lengths from 9½ to 8 inches are likewise recorded. It is quite possible that Ned Buntline found the inspiration for his presentations at the Philadelphia

World's Fair of 1876, where the attachable skeleton stock formed part of the Colt exhibit.[9] This accessory was advertised in London price lists and by B. Kittredge & Co., who offered in addition a 16 inch "carbine barrel." Each of these extras was priced at $5. The first full length catalog published by Colt's in 1888 quotes barrels over 7½ inches at one dollar for each additional inch.

Another frontier character who ordered a .45 from Colt's was John Wallace Crawford, otherwise known as "Captain Jack, the Poet Scout of the Black Hills." A Union veteran of the War Between the States and a prospector for gold in the Dakotas, he succeeded Buffalo Bill as chief scout for General Wesley Merritt in the Indian campaign of 1876. Later he took part in Buffalo Bill's Wild West Show, in the course of which his nickel-plated Peacemaker with an ivory handle purchased in February, 1881, was on display.[10] Captain Jack's verse was rather flamboyant, as these lines on the burial of "Wild Bill" Hickok exemplify: [11]

> Under the sod in the land of gold
> We have laid the fearless Bill;
> *We called him Wild, yet a little child*
> *Could bend his iron will.*
>
>   .   .   .   .
>
> Under the sod in Deadwood Gulch
> You have laid his last remains;
> No more his manly form will hail
> The red man on the plains.
>
>   .   .   .   .
>
> And while he sleeps beneath the sod
> His murderer goes free,
> Released by a perjured gaming set,
> Who'd murder you and me—

Whose coward hearts dare never meet
A brave man on the square.
Well, Pard, they'll find a warmer clime
Than they ever found out there.

The "Poet Scout," whose soubriquet supplied the title for
a book of his own verse, was unduly pessimistic about the
processes of justice. Jack McCall, who killed Wild Bill on

From Hartley & Graham Catalog, 1892

Courtesy of the Bella C. Landauer Collection in the New-York Historical Society

August 2, 1876, was, to be sure, released by the "miners'
court" of Deadwood. His plea was self-defense, although he
shot the deceased in the back of the head while Wild Bill was
dealing a poker hand. But McCall was later tried for the killing in the U. S. District Court at Yankton, convicted by a
jury and hung for murder.[12]

An identified purchaser in 1885 of a silver-plated Peacemaker, one of the first to have a bull's head carved on the
pearl handle, was Granville Stuart, a pioneer gold miner and
cattleman in Montana. His journal [13] mentions the "pearl-
handled six shooter" as part of a cowboy's trappings. Perhaps
he felt the need of one when riding range in July, 1884, he

came upon the camp of "Rattle Snake Jake" and another sus-
pected rustler. Each was "wearing two forty-four Colt revolvers and a hunting knife" and had a Winchester nearby.
Nothing happened to Stuart at this chance meeting, but both
desperadoes were killed next day when they tried to shoot up
the village of Lewistown.

The principal competitor and eventual partner of Buffalo
Bill in wild west shows was Gordon W. Lillie,[14] appearing under the professional name of "Pawnee Bill." A feature of his
performances was the shooting of glass balls thrown in the air,
the secret of the marksmanship being the use of unrifled revolvers firing bird shot. Purchase by Major Lillie of several
pair of Frontier .44s with "smooth-bore barrels, slightly
choked," is recorded in 1891, the year after his "Frontier Exhibition" was started. Pairs of pearl-handled Peacemakers
were inscribed in 1902 and again in 1906 "Presented to Pawnee Bill by the Colt Co." In 1895 the dean of wild west show
business himself is recorded as the recipient of a Special Target single action with pearl handle and gold-plated cylinder,
on the backstrap of which was inlaid "Col. Wm. F. Cody"
and on the right side "Buffalo Bill."

X

VARIATIONS
AND TARGET TYPES

THE only exception to consecutive numbering of all Model "P" revolvers, regardless of calibre, applies to those designed for the .44 rimfire Henry cartridge, of which about 1,900 were manufactured and numbered in a series by themselves. These were made between 1875 and 1880, and differed from all others in their hammer, which was made to strike the top rather than the center of the cartridge. The type is little known but its chambering for .44 calibre rimfire is confirmed not only in the old shipping records but in early broadsides of the Colt single action, which stated "This style of pistol is also made to use the cartridges manufactured for the Winchester Rifle of .44 calibre of both models, central and rim fire." The rifle last referred to was the rimfire 1866 Winchester, to the ammunition of which certain types of the altered Army Model of 1860 and of the open-top model of 1872 were also adapted. In 1874 advertisements [1] of the Union Metallic Cartridge Company, the flat nosed rimfire cartridge made for these pistols is called ".44 C. and W., adapted to Colt's new B. L. Army pistol, and Winchester carbine and rifle."

In 1878 the Model "P" in .44-40 Winchester centerfire was introduced, styled the "Frontier Six-Shooter," and its immediate popularity undoubtedly contributed to the high volume of production already noted for the early 1880s. Next to be introduced was the .41 calibre centerfire in 1885, followed by the .38 the next year and the .32 in 1887. The last two were chambered in several different styles for Colt and Smith & Wesson loads and for the Winchester rifle cartridges of .38-40 and .32-20. In 1888 the single action was chambered for the .22 R.F. All the calibres already mentioned in this paragraph are listed for the single action in the Colt catalog for 1888, as are likewise the .44 Russian and the .44 target and gallery. The .22 calibre was not listed in catalogs after 1890.

Colt's Single Action .44 Rimfire
Courtesy of H. H. Sefried

Up to serial 165,000 whose year of manufacture was 1896, the Model "P" was designed for black powder, but all single actions above that number were adapted for smokeless. The adaption consisted in reducing and standardizing at .060 inches the space for the cartridge case head between the cylinder and recoil plate, so as to preclude blowout of the cartridge cap because of increased powder pressure. No increase in metal of the cylinder or barrel was found necessary. About the same time the cylinder pin screw, which had entered from underneath the frame forward, was changed to a spring catch working from the left side, thus permitting the cylinder to be removed without the use of a screwdriver. A general change in rifling, equalizing the width of lands and grooves, came later, as did the advent of heat treatment of the metal. The 1906 Colt catalog was the first to contain a guarantee of all arms for use with either black or smokeless powder in standard factory loaded ammunition.

Except for the Army issues, which had one piece wooden grips, the Model "P" was furnished after 1882 with two piece hard rubber handles, a rampant colt in an oval medallion being impressed on either side of them at the top. Until 1896 the rubber grips were also embossed below the screw holding them together with an American eagle. It was of course always possible to specify grips of wood or other material. The earliest Peacemakers had a round head on the ejector rod; this was soon changed to an oval and less obtrusive shape. About 1901 the blade front sight of the single action was substantially enlarged. Standard barrel lengths were 7½, 5½ and 4¾ inches with ejector, and 3½ and 4 without. The short lengths were offered in the Colt catalogs from 1888 to 1898. A few pistols without ejectors but with barrels as short as 2½ inches and as long as 4½ were also recorded in the shipping books. By special order the ejector was occasionally omitted even on the longer barrels.

Markings of the various types and calibres of Model "P" differ considerably. All have "COLT'S PT. F. A. MFG C⁰ HARTFORD CT. U.S.A." stamped on the top of the barrel reading from the muzzle. Pistols exported to England are sometimes marked in addition "DEPOT 14 PALL MALL LONDON," permission for this stamping having been granted by the Commissioners of Her Majesty's Customs in 1876. The patent dates Sept. 19, 1871, July 2, 1872 and (except for the earliest issues) Jan. 19. 75 appear on the lower left side of the frame in a variety of alignments. Serial numbers are found, usually though not invariably, on the frame, triggerguard, backstrap and handle (inside). Early Army issues also had a serial on the cylinder and ejector case. Numbers on the inside of the loading gate do not appear to correspond with other serials.

Apart from the various Army inspection marks previously described, the Colt factory proofmark ∇ is stamped on the upper forward section of the triggerguard on the left hand side, beginning generally about serial 217,000. The encircled rampant colt trademark stamped on the frame behind the patent dates is found commencing in the neighborhood of serial 150,000.

It is in the calibre designations on the left side of the barrel that the greatest variance occurs. The early Army issues had none, but the Peacemaker proper is generally marked "45 COLT." The Frontier Model is marked "COLT FRONTIER SIX SHOOTER 44-40," and the Bisley "(BISLEY MODEL)" followed by calibre indications such as "45 COLT." or "44 RUSSIAN CTG." The author has not examined specimens of all the different calibres mentioned herein, but is familiar with markings such as "41 COLT," "38 W.C.F," "38 COLT" and "32 W.C.F," either alone as with the regular or special target models, or preceded by the phrase "(BISLEY MODEL)." Late issues are marked "COLT SINGLE ACTION ARMY" followed by designations such as "32-20," ".38 Special," ".44 Special," "45" and ".357." Occasionally the calibre is stamped in small letters on the left side of the triggerguard.

Finish of the single action was in three main styles—"best citizens' finish" or full blued—Government finish, which was blued except for a case hardened frame and hammer, and nickel-plated. The second was used in filling Ordnance Department orders and generally supplied commercially. The first was standard for target models and could be specified in any order. Refinished arms were usually full blued. Nickel plating available from 1877 became very popular in the early days, particularly for export, but latterly saw use chiefly in fancy arms. Besides these three standard surfacings, the Colt factory supplied on special order silver, gold or copper plated

Colt's Bisley Target and two Special Target Models. Middle specimen, with British proofmarks, belonged to Walter Winans and is marked "w.w/.450" on backstrap. Revolver with extra long handles is stamped "DEPOT 14 PALL MALL LONDON" on barrel

Courtesy of Herbert Ader

arms or parts, a browned finish or a dark dull one known as "dead," and "soft" or "white" arms for hardening or engraving elsewhere. Machine engraving of foliate designs was also available in several grades, depending on price.

An unusual variation in the Model "P" is one with serial numbers 330,001 to 331,480, dating from about 1915. These are standard in every respect except that they have cylinders originally made for the double action Army Model of 1878. When that model was discontinued about 1910, there remained on hand at the factory a quantity of cylinders with the same dimensions as those of Model "P," except that the fluting on the cylinder extended further back and milling for cylinder stops was lacking. This lot of cylinders was utilized to complete some 1,500 single actions, a notation that the above listed serial numbers were made "with D. A. cylinders" being found in the shipping records. A few others were used later and noted as having "O.S. [old style] Cylinder." These variations can be identified by their longer fluting.

More readily distinguished and a variation so common as to constitute a separate type is the Bisley, made on the Model "P" frame with a new design of hammer, trigger, and handle. Named for the English town famed for its international target shooting contests, this arm was manufactured between 1895 and 1912 mainly for marksmen. Years before the official advent of this model, Colt's had been making on special order Model "P" revolvers with handles longer than usual made of gutta percha and fitted with target sights. A special target single action distinguished by a flat top frame and target sights was listed in the 1890 and 1892 catalogs. In 1895 the Bisley appeared in the catalog of Messrs. Holland & Holland, gunmakers, of 98 New Bond Street, London, but labeled Colt's "Target Revolver—Model 1895." It was likewise advertised in the *London Illustrated News* [2] as "Colt's New '95

Model .455 Cal. Army and Target Revolver in One." Next year it was officially styled the Bisley, and is found so denominated in Colt's catalog for 1898 and Holland & Holland's catalog of 1900. Its most conspicuous feature was its large handle with sharp drop, which was combined with a low hammer and a wide curved trigger. Official introduction abroad came as if in answer to a wish expressed by a British Army officer at the same meeting of the Royal United Service Institution addressed by Colonel Fosbery, previously mentioned: [3]

What happens at Bisley is this: There are two cartridges, .450 and .455. At the 20 yards target almost everybody uses the .450 because there is slightly less recoil. Directly they come to shoot at the 50 yards target almost everybody uses .455, because they do not think the other so accurate at the longer range. . . . If our pistol makers will kindly get rid of the double action and give us a gun we can cock with our thumbs without losing our hold on the stock, and which will keep [kick] straight back, not up, they will get rid of a great part of the trouble about the recoil.

For the English market the Bisley was chambered for the English service cartridges of .450 and .455 Eley, respectively known as the Mark I and Mark II. In this it followed the Peacemaker, which was made not only in these foreign calibres but also in the Mark III of .476 Eley, and in the 1870s in the .450 Boxer and .44 German Government [4] cartridges. These loads were all much lighter than the American standard, the .450 having fourteen grains of powder and a bullet of 230 grains, the .455 eighteen grains of powder and 267 grains lead, and the .476 eighteen grains powder and 270 grains lead. The Bisley sold in much greater volume in the United States than abroad, and was chambered for the entire range of domestic centerfire cartridges from .32 calibre to .45. Barrel lengths with and without ejector were the same as for other Model "P"s.

COLT'S REVOLVERS.

Target Revolvers—1895 Model.
Shot and regulated by HOLLAND & HOLLAND if desired.
'450 or '455 bore, single action, 7½ inch barrel,
interchangeable sights, weight 2 lb. 8 oz.

PRICE ... ...   £4 7 6 to £4 17 6

       £6 0 0 to £6 10 0

Model Army Pattern Revolvers.
Shot and regulated by HOLLAND & HOLLAND.
Double action, six shot, 5½ inch barrel, regulated for the '450, '455, or '476 cartridge.

PRICE.—Blued ... ... £3 15 0 to £4 5 0

     Nickel plated ... ... £4 0 0 to £4 15 0

Frontier Revolvers.
Shot and regulated by HOLLAND & HOLLAND.
Single action, six shot, 7½ inch barrel. Regulated to shoot the '440 Magazine Rifle Cartridge, forty grains
powder, and 200 grains bullet.

The above Revolver is also made double action, to shoot the three English Government Cartridges.

PRICE.—Blued ... ... £3 2 0 to £3 12 0

     Nickel plated ... ... £3 7 6 to £3 17 6

New U.S. Service Revolvers.
Self extracting, double action, 38 calibre, 4½ inch barrel.

PRICE ... ... £3 5 0 to £3 15 0

Pocket Model.
32 calibre.

PRICE ... ... £2 10 0 to £3 0 0

From Holland & Holland Catalog, 1895

With the delisting of the Special Target single action, the Bisley appeared in the 1898 Colt catalog in a target model with flat top frame and target sights front and rear. It and its predecessor were made with a 7½ inch barrel, and though not listed in the catalogs, occasionally with one of 5½ inches. The same range of domestic and foreign calibres was available as for the conventional models, Metford rifling being sometimes supplied for the English bores. The Bisley and Bisley Target were delisted in 1912, the same year that .41 calibre was dropped for the single action. The next year .44 S & W Special was added as an available calibre for the Model "P," which in 1909 was no longer listed in .32 and in 1914 dropped for .38 Colt. These calibres for Smith & Wesson loads did not appear in Colt listings of the single action or Bisley after 1898. While the Special Target single action was not mentioned in Colt catalogs after 1892, serial numbers of specimens found indicate that this model continued to be made in a variety of calibres on special order for a long time afterwards.

The same is true of many of the calibres whose listings were discontinued in the catalogs. One calibre that was dropped and later revived (though with a different actual measurement) was .38 Colt. Beginning with the early 1920s Peacemakers of this denomination (actually .346) were made in increasing quantity, with .38 Colt Special, .38 S & W Special and .38 Special also supplied on particular order. The latter designation first appeared in the 1932 Colt catalog as a chambering which would accommodate all other .38s except .38 S & W. It became a common saying at the factory that "all .38 calibres are .35 except .38-40, which is .41."

Besides this revival of the .38, two new calibre designations were introduced in the Model "P" after World War I. The first, .45 automatic, appeared in production in 1924, though never listed in the catalogs. It was a logical development from

Variations of Colt's Single Action, above in .44 R.F. and below with
D.A. Cylinder

Courtesy of Roy S. Horton

the adaptation during the first War of the Colt "New Service"
double action revolver to the .45 automatic cartridge. Army
and Navy officers who liked to shoot the Peacemaker are said
to have suggested its chambering for service ammunition. According to the shipping records they were the principal purchasers of the arm in this new calibre. The .45 automatic cartridge needed no clip in the single action, as it could be ejected
readily by the knockout rod. Relatively few complete revolvers were made, a far greater number of special cylinders
being supplied, particularly after the inception of World War
II. It is probable that the ivory-handled single action Colt

with which General George S. Patton, Jr. adorned himself for the benefit of photographers was chambered for .45 automatic.[5]

The second new calibre for the Model "P" was .357 Magnum, first produced in 1935. Peculiarly adaptable to the heavy frame of the single action whose balance minimized the recoil developed in other models, this calibre was increasingly popular and soon ranked second only to .45 in single action production. So as not accidentally to be loaded in an arm not meant for it, the .357 cartridge was designed to require a chamber of very long dimensions. This would also accommodate the less powerful loads of the .38 Colt or S & W Special, although a cylinder made for these calibres would not take the Magnum. The history of this cartridge with its muzzle velocity of 1,515 foot seconds is well told in McHenry & Roper's *Smith & Wesson Hand Guns,* and requires no repetition here. Chambering of the Model "P" for it was first announced in the Colt catalog of 1936. That a frame originally designed in 1872 for a black powder charge with a maximum muzzle velocity of 890 foot seconds could, without increase of metal, be safely utilized for the most powerful of modern pistol cartridges is but further evidence of the rugged durability of the Peacemaker.

XI

SERIAL NUMBERS
AND SALES

MUCH may be learned from a study of the serial numbers appearing on the Model "P" and its immediate ancestors. What is noted hereafter, however, is only in the nature of an approximation, as the manner in which manufacturing records were kept and the fire and floods through which they passed preclude exact answers. Beginning with the principal percussion ancestors, it is believed that there were originally manufactured:

> 215,000 Navy Model of 1851, .36 calibre;
> 200,000 Army Model of 1860, .44 calibre;
> 38,000 Navy Model of 1861, .36 calibre.

This conclusion is based on the fact that the highest serials found for either altered or unaltered specimens are in these respective ranges. For the 1849 pocket model in .31 calibre, the top serial is even higher, in the 332,000 range, but it is known that the numbering of this model began where the 1848 pocket left off, and there is evidence also that many pocket alterations with rebated cylinders in .38 calibre were included in the same series of numbers.

Richards conversions of the 1860 Army are usually found in the 180,000-200,000 serial range, but as the original powder and ball arm was still being sold from the factory as late as 1878, the number converted was considerably less than this range might otherwise indicate. It is estimated that the num-

111

ber of Richards forty-fours with cut down cylinders and old barrels sold originally as alterations was only about 5,000, while another 2,000 or so were altered through the fitting of new barrels or barrels and cylinders. A few of these had hammers striking through a slot in the recoil plate and some were .44 rimfire, but the more common Richards conversion appears to have been .44 centerfire. It is referred to in the old shipping records as the "Army B L" and later as the "Army 44/c C F" or "Army 44/c Alt." Of course some of the Model of 1860 previously issued must have been returned to the factory for alteration, but, except for 1,000 known to have been converted in 1871 for the Ordnance Department of the United States Army at $3.50 each,[1] there is no remaining record of their number. A limiting factor is, however, that only the so-called "officers' type" of the 1860 Model seems to have been converted. Issues during the War of this type, the breechplate of which was not milled for an attachable shoulder-stock, were relatively few. The Richards conversion was sold from 1871 through 1877 and in its rarer form with new barrel was often renumbered. Serials on these are found up to the 7,000 range, but this is considered more indicative of the over-all number altered than of those having new barrels. Cuts of the Richards .44 in advertisements and catalogs of the 1870s suggest twelve slots in the periphery of the cylinder instead of the six that the author has found in every specimen examined. Yet a few actual examples of the twelve slotter are reported by collectors to exist.

Following the Richards conversion, the next model developed has become known as the Army Model of 1872. It was of open top design with the barrel secured to the frame by a wedge, but all parts were newly fabricated. Made from 1872 to 1876, it was numbered in a series of its own, up to about

5,300. Specimens from No. 1 to No. 4796 are known to the author. The Model 1872 was originally designed for .44 rimfire, but some were altered to centerfire by changes in the hammer. It is referred to in the old shipping records as the "Army 42/c," perhaps because .42 inches was the measurement between the lands of the Henry rifle, whose rimfire cartridge this revolver was designed to use. Early specimens had handles of Navy size with brass or iron straps; later ones were of iron with Army dimensions. The 1871 and 1872 patent dates of the Richards conversion appear on the frames of the latter.

The separate serials of the .44 rimfire solid frame single action (designated "Army 44/c R F S F" in the old shipping records) have already been discussed. The highest of these was in the 1800s, but the majority in this range were made over in 1888 to chamber .22 rimfire. The only recorded example of the single action in .32 rimfire was also numbered in the 1800s. Apart from these rimfire types, all revolvers made on the Model "P" frame were numbered in the same series. Those sold commercially began in the 8,000 range, following the first Army order, except for about 375 with lower serials. These are accounted for by the fact that the first commercial sale of the Peacemaker took place on September 2, 1873, when a few were sold to Schuyler, Hartley & Graham, and other such limited sales preceded the completion of the first Army order for 8,000 in June, 1874. Thereafter Army orders and commercial sales were filled as they occurred, with no particular allocation of serial numbers. The Peacemaker was first listed in the old shipping records as the "Army A," then as "Army A Govt." and ultimately as "Army 45/c." It was first sold to the Government at $13 each, later reduced to $12.50. The initial list price to the public was $17. After advancing to $20, it dropped by 1888 to $16.

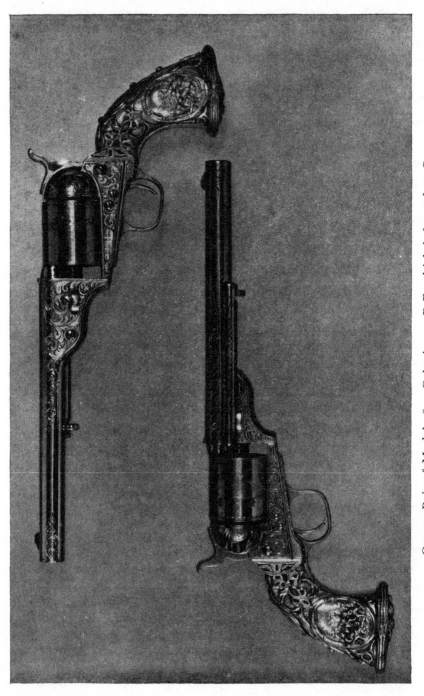

Ornate Pair of Model 1872 Colts in .44 R.F. which belonged to General Aureliano Rivera of Mexico, who served during the administration of President Porfirio Díaz.

The principal wholesalers initially handling the Peace-maker were the five so-called Colt Allies, Schuyler, Hartley & Graham, H. & D. Folsom, J. P. Moore's Sons and Spies & Kissam of New York, and B. Kittredge & Co. of Cincinnati. They formed a pool which in 1875 and 1876 bought altogether 12,000 Peacemakers at $10.50 each, a price lower than that made to the Government. This special discount may have been occasioned by the fact that the Allies were providing all the periodical advertising for Colt's, not only of the Peace-maker but for its other pistols. A letter of April 3, 1876, to the Allies explained Colt's sales policy as follows:

We do not propose to offer the 45/cal Army in opposition to the Allies but rather to encourage and strengthen their efforts in all cases. Many of our sales are to soldiers and private individuals and where we are asked to give prices to the trade it is always list price with discount of 20 & 10% for a fixed quantity cash COD and in such cases we usually refer the parties to the Allies stating that they may be "able to" offer them more favorable terms. . . . We will not consent at the present time to any arrangement that would exclude us from furnishing the "Peacemaker" to those who may favor us with a call for one or more.

By the 1880s the Allies ceased to function collectively and the number of jobbers and dealers had expanded to include among others the Simmons Hardware Co. and E. C. Meacham Arms Co. of St. Louis, Hibbard Spencer & Co. of Chicago, Schoverling, Daly & Gales, Herman Boker & Co. and Meyer & Geiger of New York, Wexell & Degress of New York and Mexico City, N. Curry & Bro. of San Francisco, William R. Burkhard of St. Paul, John P. Lower of Denver, J. C. Pet-mecky of Austin, Texas, Charles Hummel & Son of San Antonio, A. J. Anderson of Ft. Worth, E. K. Tryon Jr. & Co. and Jos. C. Grubb & Co. of Philadelphia, and Wm. Read & Sons of Boston. The Winchester Repeating Arms Co. did a

large export business in Colt single actions, many of them
nickel-plated, and many fancy arms were ordered by A. Combaluzier, a dealer in Mexico City. Colt's London Agency handled trans-Atlantic business and domestic agencies were established in New York and San Francisco. Enlargement of the
roster of dealers was prompted by applications such as the
following of November 19, 1878, from the Simmons Hardware Co.:

> Our company are now doing a very large Gun, Pistol & Sporting
> Goods business and are buying of others very largely of your Pis-
> tols—for example have bought over a thousand of your Army this
> year and could have sold double the quantity if it had been any
> object to us. . . . We keep twenty regular travellers on the road
> besides three special Gun & Pistol men and in view of these facts
> we write to ask if you cannot put us on the same footing as your
> New York friends and Kittredge of Cincinnati. Our city (St.
> Louis) is probably next to New York the best distributing point
> in this country for your goods and if we are to handle them with
> spirit and earnestness we must be put on the ground floor or we
> can have no heart in the matter.

In the 1890s the list of dealers also included such firms as
Powell & Clement of Cincinnati, J. P. Lovell Arms Co. of
Boston, Charles J. Godfrey of New York, W. B. Belknap &
Co. of Louisville, Farwell-Ozmun, Kirk & Co. of St. Paul,
Janney Semple Hill & Co. of Minneapolis, Richards & Con-
over of Kansas City, Marshall Wells Hardware Co. of Duluth,
Winnipeg, Spokane and Portland, Browning Brothers of Og-
den, Utah, Babcock & Miles of Billings, Montana, E. J. Post
& Co. of Albuquerque, Walter Tips of Austin, Texas, Bering-
Cortes Hardware Co. of Houston, The El Paso Saddlery Co.,
the Salt Lake Hardware Co., and Montgomery Ward & Co.

The next decade saw a greatly expanded list of dealers
usually handling lots of less than fifty pistols, which since the
commencement of Army purchases had been the standard

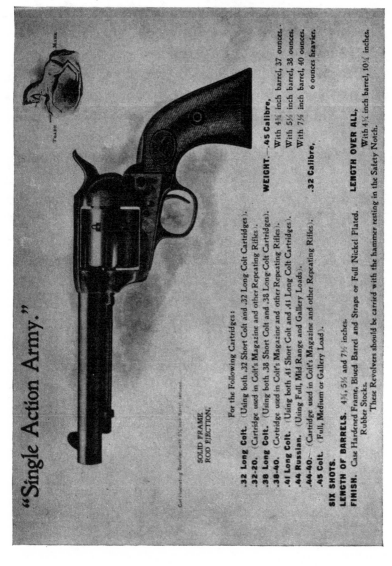

"Single Action Army."

SOLID FRAME.
ROD EJECTION.

For the Following Cartridges:

.32 Long Colt. (Using both .32 Short Colt and .32 Long Colt Cartridges).

.32-20. (Cartridge used in Colt's Magazine and other Repeating Rifles).

.38 Long Colt. (Using both .38 Short Colt and .38 Long Colt Cartridges).

.38-40. (Cartridge used in Colt's Magazine and other Repeating Rifles).

.41 Long Colt. (Using both .41 Short Colt and .41 Long Colt Cartridges).

.44 Russian. (Using Full, Mid Range and Gallery Loads).

.44-40. (Cartridge used in Colt's Magazine and other Repeating Rifles).

.45 Colt. (Full, Medium or Gallery Load).

SIX SHOTS.

LENGTH OF BARRELS. 4¾, 5½ and 7½ inches.

FINISH. Case Hardened Frame, Blued Barrel and Straps or Full Nickel Plated. Rubber Stocks.

These Revolvers should be carried with the hammer resting in the Safety Notch.

WEIGHT.—.45 Calibre,

With 4¾ inch barrel, 37 ounces.
With 5½ inch barrel, 38 ounces.
With 7½ inch barrel, 40 ounces.

.32 Calibre, 6 ounces heavier.

LENGTH OVER ALL,

With 4¾ inch barrel, 10¼ inches.

From Colt's Catalog, 1902

number for a box. Notable among such dealers was a group
on the West Coast who presumably supplied customers in
Alaska. These included Schwabacher & Co. of Seattle and the
Seattle Hardware Co., Honeyman Hardware Co. of Portland,
Oregon, and the following firms in San Francisco: Baker &
Hamilton, Dunham Carrigan & Hayden Co., Golcher Bros.
and Pacific Hardware & Steel Co. Orders from Canadian firms
such as Miller Morse & Co. and J. H. Ashdown Hardware
Co. of Winnipeg, Manitoba, Revillon Freres of Edmonton,
Alberta, Charles E. Tisdall of Vancouver, and Wood Val-
lance & Co. of Hamilton, Ontario, indicate that they also
figured in the Klondike trade. Along the border and in
Mexico a third group evidenced the expanding demand for
the Peacemaker in this area: L. Zeckendorf & Co. and A. Steinfeld & Co. of Tucson, A. Deutz & Bros. of Laredo, Ketelson
& Degetau of Juarez, Langstroth & Co. of Monterey, F. Willmanns & Co. of Durango, Krakauer, Zork & Moye of Chi-
huahua, Juan H. Kipp of Guadalajara, and Quintana Hermanos of Mexico City. It would not be feasible to list all the
dealers of the 1900s, the following names in addition to many
already mentioned being selected merely because of their
euphony or location: Blish, Mize & Silliman of Atchison,
Kansas, Bonebrake Hardware & Implement Co. of El Reno,
Oklahoma, H. S. Bettes of Paris, Texas, J. B. Crook & Co. of
New York, Coeur d'Alene Hardware Co. of Wallace, Idaho,
Gonzales & Schaper of Galveston, Harper & Reynolds of Los
Angeles, C. M. McClung & Co. of Knoxville, Tennessee,
McIntosh Hardware Co. of Albuquerque, Missoula Mercan-
tile Co. of Missoula, Montana, Rector & Wilhelmy of Omaha,
Salem G. Le Valley Co. of Buffalo, N. Y., Shapleigh Hard-
ware Co. of St. Louis, Speer Hardware Co. of Ft. Smith,
Arkansas, Stauffer Eshleman & Co. of New Orleans, Von

Lengerke & Antoine of Chicago and Abercrombie & Fitch of New York.

With the entry of the United States into World War I, production of the Model "P" dropped for the first time below one thousand per annum. The days of great demand were over and the single action was fast becoming a show piece, rather than a weapon of utility. After the first War,

Skeletonized example of the Peacemaker

Courtesy of Colt's Manufacturing Company

though the number of presentation orders increased relatively, the size of sales seldom exceeded one or two pistols at a time. While still selling through jobbers and dealers, the Colt Company was in effect doing a retail, custom trade in the Peacemaker.

Only two exceptions to this diminution in volume have been noted—the arm continued to be ordered by Western police and ranger forces, particularly in Texas, and it enjoyed a steady popularity in Hollywood. As late as 1927 the single action was supplied in quantity to the San Antonio police department, and a decade later to the police of Beaumont, Texas. All through the '20s and '30s numerous single orders from county sheriffs and chiefs of police were recorded. Motion picture studio purchases were not always direct, but names like Lasky, Fox, Columbia, and Republic recur in the shipping records and Western stars like William S. Hart and Tom Mix were devotees. In another line of show business substantial users were Miller Brothers of Marland, Oklahoma, proprietors of the 101 Ranch.

The last considerable purchase of the Model "P" had dramatic aspects also. On June 18, 1940, the British Purchasing Commission, acting through the Winchester Repeating Arms Company, bought 108 single actions of .45 calibre, 36 of .38 and 19 of .357 Magnum. They were all the Model "P"s in these calibres on hand at the Colt factory. Obsolete for military purposes though they were, the British Government lost no time in adding them, with 200 rounds apiece supplied by Winchester's, to its slim store of arms against expected invasion. Had the Battle of Britain not been won in the skies, the Peacemaker would thus have figured in the fight promised by Churchill "in the fields and in the streets."

XII

VOLUME OF PRODUCTION BY CALIBRES

IN A PREVIOUS chapter the dates of introduction of the various calibres of the Model "P" have been given, together with the chronology of delisting. For thirty years after its initial appearance in 1873 the .45 remained the most popular of all calibres, although run a close second, if Army orders are disregarded, by the .44 in the 1880s and early 1890s. This was the heyday of the .44-40 Winchester rifle, when the idea of carrying a pistol taking the same cartridge had wide appeal. The same consideration undoubtedly accounted for the strong showing of the .38-40, which ran third in popularity until about 1900, when it eclipsed the .44, passing the .45 also in 1903. It never was headed again by the .44, which declined steadily in favor, but in 1908, at the end of the second great production period of the single action, the .45 regained a place ahead of the .38-40. Meanwhile, however, the .32-20, another rifle calibre, had grown impressively in volume, passing the .38-40 in 1905 to lead all bores. This pre-eminence was fairly short lived—by 1911 the .32-20 had dropped back of the .45 to take third place behind the .38-40.

One other calibre deserves mention as having a popularity more considerable than generally supposed—the .41. While having exactly the same bore dimensions as the .38-40, its chambering differed. For twenty years following its introduction in 1885, the .41 enjoyed a steady demand of some 500 or more a year, not until 1900 giving up fourth place to the .32-20. Of the less popular calibres of the Model "P," .38 Colt was consistently the leader. In very slight demand were the several Smith & Wesson loads, except for .44 S & W Special. Competitive factors only can account for these calibres remaining in production at Colt's.

As regards the Bisley, the popular choice in calibres showed a very different pattern. Identical ammunition with a rifle was but a minor consideration for target shooters, who did, however, show a marked preference for the smaller bores. Except for the first couple of years after its introduction in 1895, the Bisley was in greatest demand in .38-40, followed by .32-20 which in 1903 took a slight lead. This precedence was maintained until discontinuance of the model in 1912. As between the .45 and .44, there was only a slight preference, neither attaining much over half the popularity of the .32-20, though perhaps double that of the .41. The .38 Colt again made a better showing than the remainder, while the Smith & Wesson loads, except possibly for .44 Russian, were in negligible demand.

Explanation of the discontinuance of the Bisley, a special favorite with collectors nowadays, may be found in the steady decline in sales of the model commencing in 1908. At the peak of its popularity some 4,000 (relatively ¼ of total Model "P" production) had been sold yearly. By 1912 this volume had shrunk to under a thousand. Colt's had developed faster shooting double action target revolvers and the Bisley was on the way to becoming a collector's gun. A similar fate was to overtake the conventional single action, but not until two wars and some thirty years later.

Production of special target models, both in the single

PRICE LIST

OF

COLT'S REVOLVING AND BREECH-LOADING FIRE-ARMS, &c.

Colt's Revolvers have been supplied to the English, American, Russian, Prussian, Austrian, French, Dutch, Turkish, and Egyptian Governments : to those of Brazil, China, Chili ; to the various Governments of the English Colonies, &c., &c.

THE PRIZE MEDALS OF 1855, 1862, 1867 AND 1873 WERE AWARDED TO THE COLT'S COMPANY.

COLT'S NEW PATENT BREECH-LOADING CENTRAL-FIRE GOVERNMENT REVOLVER, '450 Bore.

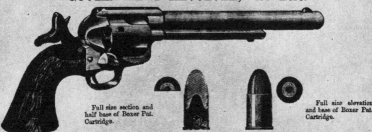

Full size section and
half base of Boxer Pat.
Cartridge.

Full size elevation
and base of Boxer Pat.
Cartridge.

This Pistol, which has recently been exclusively adopted by the United States Government, after a most severe competitive trial with the best Revolvers made, has been found to be the best Pistol extant for military purposes. It surpasses all others in length of range, accuracy of fire, penetration, in simplicity and durability of construction. It can be easily loaded and unloaded in the dark and can be carried with perfect safety when loaded. It far surpasses, in quality and workmanship, the numerous cheap Revolving Pistols which now flood the market. It takes the '45 Calibre English Government Boxer Cartridge.

Price, £5 each. In case complete, £6. Cartridges, 8s. per 100. Holster, Belt, and Pouch, £1.

Extract from Government Report on trials with Breech-loading Revolvers.

Colt's Revolver was first fired three hundred rounds with service ammunition, allowing it to cool after each hundred rounds. No difficulty was experienced with it, and only one cartridge failed to explode. This one was found to be defective in fulminate.

The Revolver was then laid in the snow, water poured over it, and it was allowed to remain in the weather three days and nights. When taken up again it was rusted considerably, but worked perfectly. It was again fired up to two hundred rounds, with two cartridges failing to explode. One of these exploded at second trial and the other with the punch and hammer.

As the reports on the several models of Revolvers using the metallic ammunition plainly show the superiority of the Colt's Revolver (last model) over all others tried, the Chief of Ordnance has been authorized by the War Department to purchase 8,000 of those Arms for the use of the cavalry arm of the service.—*Ordnance Office, June 26th, 1873.*

NOTE.—The contract with this Company was extended April 30th, 1874, to include 2,000 additional Pistols, making 10,000 in all, and the whole, of the United States Cavalry has now been armed with them.

ATTACHABLE SKELETON CARBINE STOCK, for the same, £1 10s.

This Attachable Stock can be easily fitted to any of these Pistols by simply re-placing the original hammer screw by one with projecting ends, which is supplied with the Attachment. The Pistol then becomes an efficient Carbine.

Colt's London Price List, 1876

Courtesy of John Hintlian

action and Bisley, was relatively light. Not more than 100 of either kind were sold in any year. Volume by calibres was quite unrelated to standard issues, in fact in the less popular bores the special targets were, if anything, more numerous. This was particularly the case with Smith & Wesson loads. .455 Eley was the calibre having the largest production in the Bisley Target, and .38 Colt for the Special Target.

While a great number of calibres are listed for the Model "P," the varying dimensions of the bore are less numerous than those of the chamber, and in the latter there are even duplications. Thus, barrels in five sizes sufficed for some fifteen calibre designations, the same barrel being usable, for example, in the .38 Colt Special and the .357 Magnum, or in the .45 and the .455 Eley. Chambering was the same for several of the thirty-eights, one cylinder being made to take .38 Colt, and .38 Colt Special or .38 S & W Special. The only difference in fact between the last two was in the shape of the bullet, that of the Colt having a flat nose. A larger size cylinder was made which would take all three of the English calibres of .450, .455 and .476. Occasionally a pistol was sold with an extra cylinder of different chambering, as for instance, .45 and .45 automatic or .455 Eley. Tolerance in bore dimensions was very generally one-thousandth of an inch, but dimensions sometimes changed in the development of a calibre. Thus the bore of the .38 Colt, originally .362, and filled by an expanding base bullet, was eventually reduced in diameter to .346. A table of measurements is on page 127.

The author has compiled another table of the various calibres and styles in which the Model "P" was made, from 1873 down to 1940. This is based on the shipping records and correlated with the schedule of serial numbers, but it is not official in the sense that the Company supplied any totals.

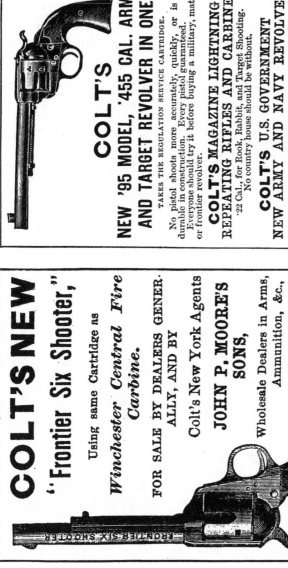

COLT'S NEW '95 MODEL, '455 CAL. ARMY AND TARGET REVOLVER IN ONE

TAKES THE REGULATION SERVICE CARTRIDGE.

No pistol shoots more accurately, quickly, or is as durable in construction. Every pistol guaranteed. Everyone should try it before buying a military, match, or frontier revolver.

COLT'S MAGAZINE LIGHTNING REPEATING RIFLES AND CARBINES.

·22 Cal., for Rook, Rabbit, and Target Shooting. No country house should be without.

COLT'S U.S. GOVERNMENT NEW ARMY AND NAVY REVOLVER.

COLT'S NEW POCKET EJECTOR REVOLVER is the best made.

Price List Free.

COLT'S FIREARMS MFG. CO.,
26, Glasshouse Street, Piccadilly Circus, W.

COLT'S NEW "Frontier Six Shooter,"

Using same Cartridge as

Winchester Central Fire Carbine.

FOR SALE BY DEALERS GENERALLY, AND BY

Colt's New York Agents

JOHN P. MOORE'S SONS,

Wholesale Dealers in Arms, Ammunition, &c.,

302 BROADWAY, NEW YORK.

Wholesale lists on receipt of business card.

Advertisements from the *Army and Navy Journal*, 1878, and the *Illustrated London News*, 1895

For the count of each calibre the author must take sole responsibility, whether the result be one or in the thousands. In this effort to supply an accurate answer to "how many," an adding machine was used and several hundred hours were put in on the job. One thing is very evident from this study—that a representative collection of Model "P"s would be numerous indeed, and as difficult to complete as any other kind of arms group.

Calibre	Bore Diameter	Chamber Diameter
.32 Colt	.304-.305	.320
.32 S & W	.304-.305	.3405 to .314
.32-20	.304-.305	.3547 to .314 bottled
.32-44	.310-.311	.351 to .322
.38 S & W	.350-.351	.389 to .362
.38-44	.350-.351	.389 to .362 but longer
.38 (Colt) to 1914 . .	.356-.357	.381 to .359
.38 Colt (after 1922) .	.346-.347	.381 to .359
.38 Colt Special . . .	.346-.347	.381 to .359
.38 S & W Special . .	.346-.347	.381 to .359
.357 Magnum . . .	.346-.347	.381 to .359 but longer
.38-.40	.394-.395	.471 to .401 bottled
.41	.394-.395	.413 to .4103
.44-40	.419-.420	.472 to .428 bottled
.44 Russian	.419-.420	.459 to .4325
.44 S & W Special . .	.419-.420	.459 to .4325 but longer
.44 S & W	.419-.420	.442
.45	.444-.445	.4873 to .4555
.45 Automatic . . .	.444-.445	.493 to .443
.450 Eley	.444-.445	.4808 to .4555
.455 Eley	.444-.445	.4815 to .456
.476 Eley	.476-.477	.4829 to .4752

Calibre (Centerfire except as noted)	Volume			
	Single Action	S.A. Target	Bisley	B. Target
.22 Rimfire	107	93	—	—
.32 Rimfire	1	—	—	—
.32 Colt	192	24	160	44
.32 S & W	32	30	18	17
.32-44	2	9	14	17
.32-20 Winchester (also styled .32 Colt rifle)	29,812	30	13,291	131
.38 Colt (to 1914)	1,011	122	412	96
.38 Colt (after 1922)	1,365	—	—	—
.38 S & W	9	39	10	5
.38 Colt Special	82	7	—	—
.38 S & W Special	25	—	2	—
.38-44	2	11	6	47
.357 Magnum	525	3	—	—
.380 Eley	1	3	—	—
.38-40 Winchester (also styled .38 Colt rifle)	38,240	19	12,163	98
.41	16,402	91	3,159	24
.44 Smoothbore	15	—	1	—
.44 Rimfire	1,863	—	—	—
.44 German	59	—	—	—
.44 Russian	154	51	90	62
.44 S & W	24	51	29	64
.44 S & W Special	506	1	—	—
.44-40 Winchester (also styled .44 Colt rifle)	64,489	21	6,803	78
.45	150,683	100	8,005	97
.45 Smoothbore	4	—	2	—
.45 Automatic	44	—	—	—
.450 Boxer	729	89	—	—
.450 Eley	2,697	84	5	—
.455 Eley	1,150	37	180	196
.476 Eley	161	2	—	—
Total	310,386	917	44,350	976	356,629

XIII

PATENTS AND PIRATES

IT HAS been stated that the design of the Peace-maker is derived from Charles B. Richards' patent of July 25, 1871,[1] which covered the conversion to cartridge loading of the Army Model of 1860. Other dates, however, are found on the frame of the Model "P," September 19, 1871, a succeeding but inapposite Richards patent, being listed with one or two more. The later dates represent patents taken in the name of William Mason on July 2, 1872, and January 19, 1875,[2] and assigned, as was Richards', to the Colt Company. They covered minor improvements only, the patent of 1875 being the first whose drawings illustrated the Model "P" in its definitive form.

The Richards patent describes and illustrates quite fully the means of converting "an ordinary Colt revolver" to load metallic cartridges at the rear of the cylinder, but its actual claims are far more limited in scope. This was of course be-cause many basic features of a cartridge revolver were already in the public domain. Thus, for instance, the general system of revolving and locking the cylinder through cocking the hammer was open to general use on the final expiration in 1857 of Samuel Colt's basic patent of 1836. Likewise, a cyl-inder with chambers bored from end to end, an essential element for a rear-loading cartridge revolver and patented by Rollin White in 1855, became of free use in 1869. Several other features were expressly disclaimed by Richards as new,

128

An Imitation (unmarked) and a Variation (.44 R.F.) of Colt's Single
Action

Courtesy of Roy S. Horton

to wit "the use of a breechplate behind a bored through
cylinder, or of its gate, or of a cased ejector lying alongside
the barrel."

These disclaimers evidently referred to the ejecting devices
of prior patentees. A breechplate behind a bored through
cylinder was described in Rollin White's patent of 1855 and
hence was no longer a novelty. However, on April 2, 1867,
an inventor named Reuben W. Drew had patented a loading
gate which opened backwards on a hinge, and a tubular
ejector moving through a side projection of the barrel
(63,450). Another type of ejector sliding along the forward
extension of the center pin was patented by Gilbert H. Har-

rington on February 7, 1871 (111,534). Richards' design avoided infringing Drew's by having the loading gate swing sideways, and by placing a sliding ejector rod inside a fixed housing along the barrel. In the latter device the retracting spring was compressed by the movement of the rod, whereas in Drew's the spring was activated by the tube itself. This variation, although not claimed as patentable, was evidently adequate for the purpose. An interest in Drew's patent was acquired by Daniel B. Wesson in 1874,[3] but no evidence has been found of his having claimed an infringement.

When early specimens of the Richards conversion reached Colt's London agency in November, 1871, British patent counsel found that the spring bolt of the loading gate infringed a patent held by John Adams.[4] As may be observed in Richards' drawings dated July 25, 1871, his bolt and spring were housed within the gate and pressed against its hinge. Negotiations were initiated by counsel for a license under the Adams patent, but these apparently fell through when Adams surmised that the applicant was a principal competitor in the making of military revolvers. A change in Colt's design therefore became necessary, which explains the rather cumbersome external spring and screw securing the loading gate of most Richards conversions. This substitute was carried over into the Model of 1872, but in the Peacemaker the problem was solved by placing the spring bolt in the frame rather than in the gate.[5]

What the Richards specification actually claimed as his invention was an ejector case specially flanged to fit the rammer groove of the percussion Colt, an outlet in the ejector housing closed by the latter's attachment to the barrel, a projection in the breechplate fitting into the hammer channel, and a hinge on the end of the hand for rotating the cylinder. The latter was not actually used in produc-

Mason's Single Action Design, 1883
Courtesy of Winchester Repeating Arms Company

tion, a hand with two projections engaging the ratchet being
found more satisfactory. Thus it may be seen that the patentable features of the Richards conversion were matters of
design rather than principle. The improvements made by
Mason in the ejector housing and gate were of the same nature. An interesting aspect of the patent of January 19, 1875,
was the sleeve introduced between the cylinder and the
center pin and providing three bearing surfaces. It was evidently not deemed patentable, being mentioned in the description but not in the claims.

Despite its meager patent protection, which in any event
expired long before the popularity of the Model "P" reached

its peak, the design was never copied by other arms manufacturers in the United States. To be sure ordnance officers
who tested the Remington Model of 1875 noted that it did
not "differ essentially in principle from the Colt," but it
was not an infringement. The Winchester Repeating Arms
Company is said to have made some prototype revolvers
when it found that Colt's was embarking on the manufacture of magazine rifles in competition with the Winchester
models. An example of a .44 single action revolver resem-
bling the Frontier Model Colt about as closely as the Colt
Burgess rifle resembled the lever action Winchester is to be
found in the Winchester Museum in New Haven. This was
designed in 1883 by William Mason, the same mechanic
whose name appears on the 1872 and 1875 patents for the
Peacemaker. He was undoubtedly familiar with the state of
the art and cognizant of how little patent protection that arm
actually enjoyed. T. G. Bennett, a son-in-law of Oliver F.
Winchester, is said to have taken this and other prototype
revolvers along with him on a visit to Colt's at Hartford.
Officials there satisfied him that it would be uneconomical
for Winchester's to embark on the manufacture of pistols,
while themselves coming to the conclusion that Colt's could
not afford to continue in the lever action rifle business. This
gentleman's agreement has always since been observed.

Perhaps the most influential factor, however, in protecting
the Peacemaker from imitation at home was the development of the double action. This system was perfected in the
United States for larger calibre revolvers in the late 1870s,
having had a much earlier introduction abroad. As a rule
copyists of design are prone to reproduce something modern
rather than a pattern seemingly on the road to obsolescence.
Another protection was the substantial goodwill which Colt's
had built up over the years. When a purchaser sought a fron-

Spanish Imitation and Toy Replicas of the Peacemaker

tier type of single action revolver he thought in terms of a name that had acquired this secondary meaning—in other words of a Colt. By the same token a lever action repeating rifle would be fixed in his mind as a Winchester. Western fiction today seldom goes beyond these two names in describing the weapons of its protagonists.

Foreign-made Miniature compared to standard Peacemaker

Photograph courtesy of Winchester Repeating Arms Company

Abroad, however, and particularly in Spain and Belgium, almost exact replicas of the Peacemaker were made in unknown quantity. These are generally identifiable because of their crude finish or markings indicating national origin. Examples seen by the author were nickel-plated, and it is believed, designed for sale in Latin America. One of these in the Ulrich Museum is a close copy of the Frontier Model in .44 calibre, with 7½ inch barrel and wooden grips, marked on the barrel "ORBEA HERMANOS EIBAR." A particularly flagrant example of piracy is found in the foreign reduced-size replica of the single action in .38 calibre. This was actually stamped on the barrel "COLT'S PT F A MFG C⁰ HARTFORD CT. USA." The specimen illustrated is a fairly faithful copy of the Peacemaker on a scale of approximately 80%. It even has three patent dates (slightly garbled) stamped on the left side of the frame, but lacks interior refinements such as the inner sleeve of the cylinder and a roller bearing on the hammer. The head of the cylinder pin is dissimilar, as is the screw securing it, and the triggerguard and trigger are hardly reduced in size. There are five grooves in the rifling instead of the usual six. This type of replica is sometimes listed in dealers' catalogs as an imitation of what is styled "the miniature Colt single action made at the Springfield Armory for experimental purposes." But the fabrication at Springfield of any such model is, on the authority of no less an expert than the late Albert Foster, Jr., a myth in itself.[6]

Other miniatures of a class by themselves are the replicas in the form of small boys' toy pistols. Many of these have the characteristic lines of the Colt single action, with a cylinder that revolves, an ejector case beside the barrel and molded plastic grips reminiscent of fancy Colt arms. Features of their cap mechanism are even patented, and examples are known marked with the name "Peacemaker." Certain of these reproductions have been realistic enough to involve possessors with police regulations against the carrying of firearms. Yet the appeal which they have to the imagination of small boys is a testimonial to the significance of the originals in American history and to the fact that the Peacemaker, like the Bowie knife or the Indian war bonnet, has become one of the enduring symbols of the old West.

XIV

SIGNIFICANCE
OF THE REVOLVER

PRECEDING chapters have brought out that in the evolution of the revolver the Colt was the leader and outstanding example and that among Colts, the Peacemaker though not first in time was in many ways pre-eminent. Generically speaking, the revolver was developed in response to "a genuine need for a horseman's weapon," to quote the words of Professor Webb.[1] Initially its fire power enabled the Texas Rangers to prevail over far more numerous bands of Comanche Indians. In the Mexican War our scouting forces attained like success against horsemen who did not have this arm. Captain Walker of the U. S. Mounted Rifles went on record as saying he "would rather face 1,000 of the Enemy with 250 men, armed with *Colts Pistols* than with 1,000 men armed with the Weapons in ordinary use." [2]

Thus the percussion revolver played a significant though not decisive part in the initial expansion of our southwestern frontier, an area where it was ever to remain popular. At that time there were relatively few such arms in existence, but the next decade saw a vast increase in their production and use. The revolver crossed the plains and rounded the Horn with the Argonauts of 1849;[3] it became an official arm of the regular Cavalry, and it soon was carried very generally as a weapon of personal protection. Writing his *Texas Journey* in 1857 Frederick L. Olmsted observed "there are

probably in Texas about as many revolvers as male adults." [4]
Catlin's drawings reveal that mounted hunters found the revolver an effective instrument for killing buffalo. It was also
used to shoot bear, wolves, rattlesnakes and even deer, antelope and mountain sheep.[5]

Although its evolution began in the 15th Century, the revolver initially appeared as an arm of practical and general
use in the United States. It was the first of a sequence of
19th Century American firearms to find favor in Europe and
must be counted among the important mechanical devices
reversing the flow of invention from the Old World to the
New. Colt's revolver was introduced abroad at the London
Exhibition of 1851. It met immediately with acclaim and
competition, for patent protection had lapsed in England
and on the Continent there were many copyists.[6] Colt's single
action design was manufactured in London and purchased
by the Royal Navy, but it eventually lost ground to the perfected English double actions of Adams and Tranter. Revolvers were adopted at once by British officers in India and
South Africa. In the Crimea they were carried generally by
officers, though Lord Cardigan who led the Charge of the
Light Brigade quite forgot to draw his.[7]

With the outbreak of the War Between the States, the revolver again became preeminent as the horseman's weapon.
It was used extensively by mounted troops in both armies
and in the opinion of General Fitzhugh Lee and other Confederate leaders it was "the best arm for cavalry," not excepting the sabre or carbine.[8] In this conflict the revolver, while
to a great extent eclipsing the sabre, was no longer a new
weapon giving advantage to the side possessing it, whereas for
the first time repeating rifles and carbines played such a
part.[9] Metallic cartridges made practicable in them a fire
power far exceeding that of the percussion revolver.

"Unhorsed" by Frederic Remington, from the *Century Magazine,* January, 1892

Patent litigation retarded transformation in the United States of the military revolver into a breechloader. A restrictive patent held by Smith & Wesson was sustained in 1869, the year of its expiration, by a divided United States Supreme Court. Implicit in the decision was an answer to the query of one of the dissenting Justices as to how a weapon designed for taking life could be considered a "useful invention." [10] Congress, however, after a veto by President Grant, declined to extend the monopoly and breechloading became available for all makes of revolvers.[11] The result was undoubtedly influenced by the Army's need of an improved handarm for Indian warfare.

In its new metallic cartridge form the military size revolver enhanced its fame as an implement of the expanding frontier. In the hands of the Cavalry it was one of the weapons effective in the pacification of the Plains Indians,[12] although like the Confederates they captured and used it, too. In the hands of settlers and cattlemen the arm became an instrument, along with the Winchester and Sharps, not only of protection but utility. Keeping off marauders, human or animal, and shooting game were the prime objectives. The long corridors of the cattle drives, and the cow towns at the end of them, were policed with these weapons. Bad men and rustlers carried them too, but they and their arms were necessarily only a small fraction of the whole number. Some, like Billy the Kid, showed a preference for the latest type of short-barreled, double action revolvers suitable for either concealment or quick work at close range.[13]

Statistics confirm that the decade of 1875 to 1885 was a peak period not only in revolver design but in production. At the end of it Theodore Roosevelt wrote "of course every ranchman carries a revolver," and Frederic Remington depicted the cartridge belt and holstered pistol as part of every cowboy's dress.[14] But this period of frontier gun toting, which is the source of the romantic tradition exemplified in Hollywood westerns, was soon to come to an end. Even earlier efforts had been made to preclude the practice in settled communities. Peace officers of cattle shipping points like Abilene or Dodge City, Kansas, had enforced such disarmament in the 1870s, sometimes with fatal results.[15] By 1885 restrictive legislation had been passed in western states. Thus, for instance, Rule 1 of the XIT Ranch provided: "Six-shooters or other small fire-arms will not be permitted to be carried on the ranch. If there were no other reasons, it is forbidden by statute in the State of Texas." [16]

Although by the 1890s the revolver as an article of apparel was on the way out,[17] volume of production indicates that even the single action had yet to reach its peak of popularity. This saw military service again in the Philippine Insurrection, although supplanted by the double action for the Spanish-American War. Its greatest distribution came in the first decade of the 20th Century, reflecting a demand revived by the Klondike Rush [18] and increased use in Latin America, as well as new interest in target shooting.

Adoption of the .45 automatic pistol by the United States Army in 1911 coincided with the end of the great utility period of the single action revolver. But almost at once it became a symbolic showpiece and collector's item, following a trend started long before by the presentation to notables of fancy arms. Traditions that had grown up about the arm in its early days were thus perpetuated. The same folklore glorifies the replicas that are today made for small boys. For obvious reasons but few instances of the quick draw and the dead shot have been documented, yet the legends of them and of their practitioners, nourished in fiction for half a century, are strong and undying.

APPENDIX

THE THUER CONVERSION *

THE first factory alteration of the percussion Colt revolver for use with metallic cartridges was developed by F. Alexander Thuer, who took out his initial patent in 1868. Thuer was an employee of at least ten years' standing with the Colt Company and had been working on the development for several years. The need for a Colt arm which would take metallic cartridges had become obvious from the success of Smith & Wesson and other manufacturers in the field. As far as revolvers were concerned, the controlling factor was a patent taken out by Rollin White in 1855 on a cylinder in which the chambers were bored through from front to rear.[1] Rights under this patent had been acquired by Smith & Wesson, who utilized the cylinder for loading conventional rimfire metallic cartridges. Validity of the Rollin White patent having been sustained in litigation,[2] all other arms makers were for the time being prevented from using a bored-through cylinder.

It is not contended that Thuer's was the first method developed for converting the percussion Colt for use with metallic cartridges. Specimens of more primitive systems which probably infringed the Rollin White patent have been found.[3] The Thuer was, however, the first alteration produced at the Colt factory which was patented and marketed openly. It had the particular virtue of dual-purpose design, permitting the use of either a regular percussion-cap cylinder or one loading from the front a rimless, centerfire tapered cartridge. The essential feature of the cartridge cylinder was a plate or ring which fitted and turned independently on a tube with a ratchet on its end formed by cut-

* Reprinted from *The American Rifleman*, April, 1949, with additions.

ting down the cylinder back of the stops. The Thuer ring contained a rebounding firing pin and also a lever for ejecting the cartridges loaded by means of the regular loading lever. A turn of the ring with a thumb piece brought under the hammer either the firing pin or the ejecting lever.

While the initial patent of the Thuer system was taken out in the United States on September 15, 1868 (82,258), the British

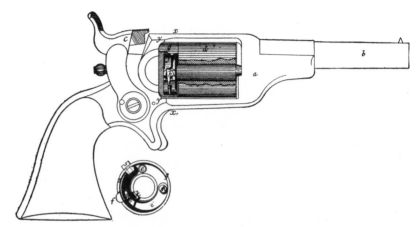

British Patent Drawing of the Thuer Alteration applied to the 1855 Side-hammer Model

patent of December 31, 1868 (3,981), is the more comprehensive. This was obtained in the name of Frederic A. K. W. Von Oppen, who was then in charge of Colt's London agency. It contains not only an elaboration of the specifications of Thuer's patent of September 15, 1868, but also a description of the cartridge-loading apparatus covered in the United States by his later patent of January 4, 1870 (98,529). The text of the American patents may be found in Haven & Belden's *A History of the Colt Revolver,* where the drawings are also reproduced.

The objective of the inventor and what he disclaimed is clearly stated in the American specifications. He defined as his primary aim a device whereby a revolver having a "cylinder capable of being loaded from the front" and "adapted for the use of loose ammunition can at small cost be changed, so that cartridges having primed metallic shells may be used." A further object was to provide "for the ejection at will of the cartridges . . . and also to provide against accidental discharge of the weapon." He disclaimed as a novelty "ejecting cartridge cases by blows of the hammer, either direct or transmitted to shells in chambers not in line with the hammer," and also "the use of a ring or plate at the rear of the chambers and containing the firing pin, when the said plate is not movable in such a way that the firing pin may be moved out of range with the hammer." The inference of the dis-

Prototype in the Arthur L. Ulrich Museum of Colt's Manufacturing Company

claimers is that their particulars were already known. The first was covered by a patent previously purchased by the Colt Company. Examples of the second are found in the primitive alterations already referred to, among which those with fixed plates were apparently in the public domain. This disclaimer may also have reference to another patent of Rollin White's taken out in 1858, which covered a detachable breech plate rotating with the cylinder and notched so the hammer struck through it.[4]

It thus is seen that the Thuer conversion was an ingenious mechanism designed to avoid the restrictions of a competitor's unexpired patents and the result of combining another's patented idea with an adaptation of features already known. In essence, the free turning of the Thuer conversion's cylinder ring was its novel aspect.

Interesting sidelights on the development of this device are cast by a diary preserved in the Arthur L. Ulrich Museum of Colt's

Manufacturing Company. This journal was kept by Major General William B. Franklin, U.S.V., who became Vice-President and General Manager of Colt's in November 1865, following the death of Elisha K. Root. Entries of April 18 and 21, 1866, record a negotiation with Rollin White, who under his assignment of patent rights (November 17, 1856) to Smith & Wesson was entitled to a royalty of twenty-five cents for each pistol manufactured. White asked $200,000 for his interest and quoted S & W as asking $600,000. This was evidently too much. Under date of January 26, 1867, General Franklin noted: "Examined Theuer's [sic] alteration. Found it good in some respects. Another one to be made." On February 11, 1867, he again looked at the "Theuer" alteration. Entries later that year indicate that Rollin White was seeking an extension of his patent of 1855, which would soon expire, and that a group of revolver manufacturers was opposing it. White meanwhile had sought to promote the purchase by Colt's of a pistol invented by Messrs. Poultney and Crispin "with a firing pin in each chamber." [5] Gen. Franklin was advised by counsel that this arm was in reality an infringement of White's patent for a bored-through cylinder, so that White's consent to its manufacture would be no protection against Smith & Wesson. In November and December, 1867, other negotiations resulted in the payment of $7,500 to Stephen W. Wood for a "patent for ejecting shells by hammer." [6] A terse entry records that the negotiators "did not talk much with Crowell, who owns another patent for ejecting by hammer." [7] It is a loss to history that the diary ends with the year 1867. The courtesy of Colt's Manufacturing Company in permitting excerpts from it to be quoted is gratefully acknowledged, as is their helpfulness in making available the letters of Baron Von Oppen later referred to.

Neither Wood's nor Crowell's designs bear much resemblance to that of Thuer. They both had cylinders adapted to front loading cartridges, but with chambers permanently closed at the rear except for small apertures to admit the hammer. In Wood's system the empty cartridge cases were ejected by direct blows of the hammer, after the barrel had been turned aside. In Crowell's design, ejection was achieved by a sliding plate fastened to the side

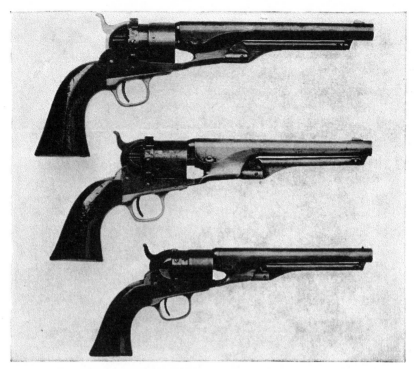

Thuer Conversions of the Army Model of 1860, Navy Model of 1861
and Police Model of 1862

of the hammer and activating a thrusting arm. It was evidently
necessary for Colt's to acquire Wood's patent because it was the
first to cover ejecting by hammer, and thus anticipated the general principle of the Thuer system. Wood's assignment to Colt's,
which included any future patents "for ejecting cartridges, or
emptying cartridge cases from the chambers of revolving fire arms
by intermediate devices operated by blows of the hammer," is recorded in the Patent Office. There is, however, no record that
Crowell's patent was ever purchased, although the Commissioner
of Patents on December 4, 1869, awarded it priority of invention
over an interference filed by Wood.[8]

General Franklin's efforts were undoubtedly spurred on by
newspaper reports of the Paris International Exhibition such as
the following from the *Illustrated London News* of August 31,
1867:

"Messrs. Colt exhibit a case of revolving pistols and rifles. These arms possess no special novelty, and indeed, are behind the age, in so far as they are none of them adapted for cartridges containing their own ignition; while on the Continent capping revolvers are as much out of date as muzzle-loading guns. Messrs. Colt have in some instances, fitted movable stocks to their pistols. If they would go a step further and adapt their pistols for self-igniting cartridges, these stocked revolvers might serve as useful arms for yeomanry regiments and various mounted corps.

"Messrs. Smith and Wesson exhibit revolving pistols and cane rifles, adapted for pistol cartridges. They are the owners of an American patent (1855) which has seriously hampered the application of self-igniting cartridges to revolvers. By this patent Messrs. Smith and Wesson hold the right in America of boring the revolving chambers from end to end.

"Although it may perhaps not be impossible to contrive a pistol adapted to self-igniting cartridges, the chambers of which are not bored from end to end, such an arrangement is necessarily a roundabout way of achieving what Messrs. Smith and Wesson, by virtue of their patent, accomplish much more simply. Thus makers of revolving pistols, desirous to go with the age and to abolish caps, must either manufacture under a license from Messrs. Smith and Wesson or must contrive some system which will render them independent of this patent, and which will yet be as cheap and efficient. To this cause we believe is to be traced the backwardness of Messrs. Colt in this matter. They are unwilling, as we understand, to purchase a license from Messrs. Smith and Wesson; and their efforts to accomplish the application of self-igniting cartridges to revolvers, without infringement of the patent referred to, have not yet met with the success which they are sanguine will ultimately crown them. In countries where Messrs. Smith and Wesson's patent does not hold the system of capping revolvers, as we have noticed, has entirely disappeared."

Notwithstanding all the efforts devoted to it, the Thuer conversion does not seem actually to have reached the public much before the expiration on April 3, 1869, of the Rollin White patent for a bored-through cylinder. In a letter from London of February 20, 1869, Baron Von Oppen reported to the Colt Company:

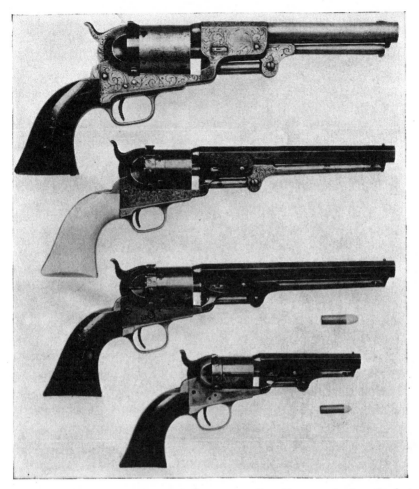

Thuer Alterations of the 1848 Dragoon, 1851 Navy and 1849 Pocket
Models

"The conversion of Army pistols is well progressing—the two
first ones altered worked well and are sold. As soon as we have
loading fixtures for Navy pistols we shall at once begin their conversion . . .

"At present we pay for the conversion of each pistol 2/6s, it
being done by a working gunmaker quite close this office . . .
We pay a further 6 d. per pistol for their conveyance to and from
the Proofhouse . . .

"I have made arrangements for having your new pistols advertized in the various Colonies and Eastern settlements . . . We have every reason to believe that these pistols will sell well in the Colonies where your nipple revolvers always were favourites.

". . . we do not think it well to advertize and bring the metallic cart. revolver to the notice of the Public in this country, till it has been submitted to the English Government, that they may receive and test the same as a novelty."

The English Government made a test of the new pistols on May 6, 1869. Colonel Dixon of the War Office reported on them as follows:

"I have had these pistols carefully examined, and had them tested by firing; The large bore or Army revolver, works very well, but the smaller bore, or Navy revolver, does not act properly—probably from some inaccuracy in the chambers or in the size of the cartridges furnished.

"The improvement effected by the alteration in these revolvers, compared with the original Colt's revolver, is particularly manifest in the Army pistol which is loaded with great facility, and the cartridge case is easily extracted by a blow from the hammer.

"The alteration is neatly arranged, and well executed, and the advantages consist in doing away with the nipples, which render the discharge of the cartridge more certain and saves time in capping. The metallic cartridges which are central fire and capable of being reloaded, and are much less liable to injury, and are more durable than the old cartridges; This is the most important feature of the improvements exhibited in this new system. Great accuracy, both in the bores and forms of chambers, as well as in the cartridges is however essential—otherwise the unexploded cartridges would shift forward, or the ends of the exploded cases jam back, and prevent the cartridges from rotating; this would render the pistol perfectly useless for the time being. . . ."

This report was not furnished to Von Oppen until July 5th, he having meanwhile written to his company on June 19th:

"From the War Office we now have a letter briefly stating that 'It is not in contemplation to convert any of the Colt pistols in store into Central Fire Breechloaders.' Privately I learn that the

Thuer Conversion of the 1851 Navy Colt, with reloading accessories

Government trials with our met. cart. pistols were on the whole satisfactory, but that the War Department cannot spare money for conversion of their Colt revolvers in consequence of the stringent measures in retrenching the expenditures adopted by the present Government; that they wish to have but one model of pistol and cartridge in the Service, keeping to the Adams's double action breechloader in use with Col. Boxer's cartridge; finally, that they consider the Colt's revolvers on hand to be scarcely worth altering, being too worn out by long use.

"This question decided we have no longer reason to postpone the intended trials with these arms in presence of experts, members of the press, etc."

These trials took place on July 10th, and were reported in *The Mechanics' Magazine* of July 23rd:

"Some public trials were recently made at the Crystal Palace with the improved revolver and ammunition, and which clearly demonstrated their value. Accuracy and penetration were all that could be desired, whilst it was abundantly proved that with a pound or two of powder and a handful of caps, a man could keep himself well supplied with central-fire cartridges for a very long time. This improvement is a step in the right direction, and will add to the fame of the already far-famed Colt revolver."

Another technical publication, *The Engineer*, was not as enthusiastic. It reported in an issue of July 16th: "We have not seen the new system thoroughly tried, and therefore we cannot express an opinion as to its success, but at present we are not inclined to think that it is the most simple contrivance that could have been suggested." This magazine later arranged a trial of the Thuer conversion at Woolwich Arsenal, with an Adams breechloader chambered for the Boxer cartridge as a basis of comparison. Its final verdict, after the careful notation "each arm was fired by its own representative" with "cartridges filled by Messrs. Eley Brothers," was: [9]

	Adams .45	Colt .44
1. Rapidity only (24 shots) . . .	1 min. 32 sec.	2 min. 10 sec.
2. Rapidity and accuracy	2 min. 18 sec.	2 min. 55 sec.
3. Accuracy (mean deviation) . .	5.92 in.	8.29 in.

NOTICE IS ALSO GIVEN to purchasers, because of the base imitations of COLT'S ARMS, advertised "on COLT'S PRINCIPLE, &c." N.B. The genuine Colt's head-ware are stamped on the barrel "Address Col. Colt, London," and bear the London proof mark on the barrel, and on the cylinder between each pair of nipple

PRICE LIST

OF

COLT'S NEW PATENT
METALLIC CENTRAL FIRE
CARTRIDGE, REVOLVERS, &c.

The Prize Medals of 1855, 1862, and 1867, were awarded to the Colt's Pat. Fire-Arms Company.

TERMS—CASH Orders from the country and abroad must be accompanied with remittance. Post Office Orders to be made payable at the PALL MALL MONEY ORDER OFFICE.

		£ s. d.
Belt or Navy Revolver, 7¼-in. barrel, 36-100 bore, Six Shot, with Wrench and Rod, weight 2lb. 9oz., carrying 50 elongated, or 86 round bullets to the pound		5 5 0
Ditto in Case complete, containing Mold, Wrench, Rod, Cartridges, Caps for re-priming the same, Loading Apparatus, &c.		6 10 0
Holster or Army Revolver, 8-in. barrel, 44-100 bore, Six Shot, with Wrench and Rod, weight 2lb. 10oz., carrying 33 elongated, or 48 round bullets to the pound.		6 0 0
Ditto in Case complete, containing Mold, Wrench, Rod, Cartridges, Caps for re-priming the same, Loading Apparatus, &c.		7 7 0
Converting Colt's **Army or Navy Revolver,** each		1 17 6
Interchangeable nipple cylinders for Belt or Holster Revolver, each.		0 15 0
Cartridges for Holster Revolvers, per 100		0 8 0
Ditto for Belt		0 7 6
Metallic Shells for either of the above sizes, per 100.		0 6 0
Caps for Re-priming Shells, per box of 250		0 2 6
Apparatus for Re-loading Shells		0 7 6

COLT'S New Patent Metallic Central Fire Cartridge Revolvers, while doing away with nipples and the necessity of capping the same, have retained all the best qualities of the original COLT'S Revolver. In length of range, accuracy of fire, force of penetration, simplicity of construction and durability, they surpass all other metallic cartridge revolvers.

By means of a simple loading apparatus used in connection with the Pistol, the Metallic Shells can be easily re-loaded and fired as often as may be required.

An interchangeable nipple cylinder can likewise be supplied with these pistols, which can then be loaded with loose powder and ball, a matter of so much importance in countries where made-up ammunition is not easily procurable.

The Shells, through the explosion of the Cartridges, do not expand and stick in the chambers of the cylinder, a common fault in other metallic cartridge revolvers, but by simply snapping the pistol when the boss of the breech ring is turned to the left of the hammer, they, or the loaded cartridges, can be more easily and rapidly ejected than this process can be performed with any pistol as yet brought out.

The above are now ready for delivery. Orders for the country and abroad will be promptly and carefully executed.

All Communications must be addressed to "COLT'S PATENT FIRE-ARMS MANFG CO.," 14, Pall Mall, London, S.W.

Colt's Fire Arms Company also contracts with the Government and others for the Alteration of Military Muzzle-loading Rifles into Breech-loaders, for the supply of New Military Breech-loading Rifles, and of all Machinery, Fixtures, Tools, &c., required for an Armoury to manufacture Small Arms on the interchangeable principle; also for the supply of the Gatling Battery Gun, as adopted by the United States Government, the Russian, and others.

Colt's London Price List, 1869

The London Times commented on these trials in its issue of October 21, 1869:

"In a competition, therefore, carried through by representatives of the two makers, on Government ground, watched by professional experimentalists, and acknowledged to be absolutely fair by all parties concerned, the Adams pistol showed its superiority to the Colt breechloader in rapidity, accuracy, rapidity combined with accuracy, and penetration, the lowest percentage of superiority being 19 per cent, the highest 41 . . . The results of the experiments last week show that intending purchasers of new pistols will be wise to buy the Adams rather than the Colt, but that those who are already in possession of Colt's revolvers may be quite content with having them converted into breechloaders on the new system."

Whether there was ever a formal introduction of the Thuer in the United States has not been established. Enough examples without foreign proofmarks are extant, however, to indicate that it was sold here. That at one time consideration of it was invited by the Ordnance Department is evident from Ordnance Memoranda No. 9, approved by the Secretary of War July 8, 1868, which stated:

"The urgency of the service not demanding the immediate introduction of pistols adapted to the use of metallic primed cartridges, and experiments not having yet determined definitely which of the numerous plans of alteration proposed is the best, the Board recommend that, prior to the adoption of any one plan, revolvers altered on the two systems of loading at the front and rear of the cylinder, respectively, be prepared for further trials at the Springfield Armory."

The Colt Company responded to this invitation on October 9, 1868, in the following letter to the Chief of Ordnance:

"We forwarded to your address today by the Adams Express Co. prepaid one of our new model army metallic cartridge pistols and sixty cartridges with printed directions for using w. This is one of the first of the kind we have produced and possibly there may be some points in the pistol or ammunition which may need slight changes. But we think there can be no doubt of the correctness of the principal and we are so well satisfied with its excel-

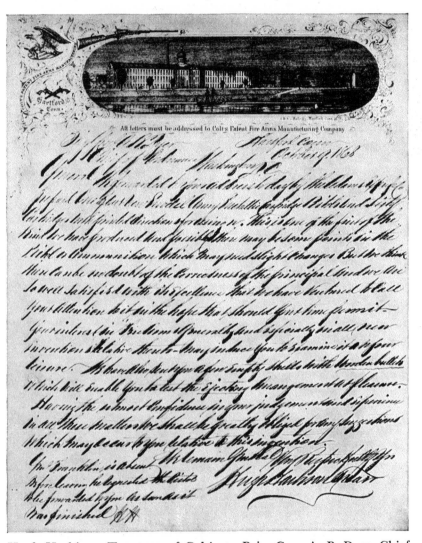

Hugh Harbison, Treasurer of Colt's, to Brig. Gen. A. B. Dyer, Chief
of Ordnance, October 9, 1868

Courtesy of The National Archives

lence that we have ventured to call your attention to it in the
hope that should your time permit—your interest in fire arms
generally and especially in all new inventions relative thereto—
may induce you to examine it at your leisure. We have also sent
you a few empty shells with *wooden bullets* which will enable you
to test the *ejecting* management at pleasure."

Very likely because of the indifferent, if not unfavorable, reception of the arm abroad, the Thuer was not pushed or advertised
in this country. Its merit of dual purpose design was but tempo-
rary, as were whatever prospects it had due to the uncertainty of
Rollin White's patent of 1855 being extended. White's application was denied by the Commissioner of Patents on April 2, 1869,
but a bill passed Congress which would have allowed a rehearing.
This was vetoed by President Grant on January 11, 1870, on the
opinion of the Chief of Ordnance that an extension would compel
the Government "to pay to parties already well paid a large royalty for altering its revolvers to use metallic cartridges." Another
bill was favorably reported by the House Committee of Patents
on February 28, 1873, but failed of enactment.[10]

In all events the Thuer was soon made obsolete by the appearance of the Richards conversion, patented on July 25, 1871.[11]
Charles B. Richards, later professor of mechanical engineering at
Yale, was then assistant superintendent of the Colt factory and his
name appears as a witness on many of its patent specifications and
drawings, including those filed by F. Alexander Thuer. Richards'
conversion, unhampered by the Rollin White patent, provided for
the loading of ordinary flanged center or rimfire cartridges at the
back of the cylinder. Its immediate success ended for good the
Thuer conversion experiment.

Of the many factors militating against the popularity of the
Thuer, the special tapered cartridge which it required was certainly one. Yet this among other factors has made it probably the
choicest and most sought after alteration as far as collectors are
concerned, though perhaps not the rarest. At least several hundred Thuers were actually made, judging from the special serial
numbers with which their altered parts are stamped. The Thuer
cartridge, incidentally, may now be even rarer than the arm itself.

From the patent specifications, it is evident that the Thuer

DIRECTIONS FOR USING
Colt's Metallic Cartridge Revolving Pistol.

TO LOAD THE PISTOL: Bring the hammer to half-cock. See that the boss ot projection on the ring in rear of the cylinder is moved in position to the *right* of the hammer. Hold the Pistol in the left hand, muzzle upwards, thumb and fore-finger grasping the cylinder, hammer to the left, butt resting on the breast. Insert the cartridges and ram them *home* in the usual manner. The Pistol is fired in the ordinary way.

TO EJECT THE SHELLS: Move the boss on the ring in rear of the cylinder to the *left* of the hammer. Then cock and snap the pistol, until all of the shells are ejected. Then move the boss on the ring back to the *right* of the hammer, and the pistol is ready for reloading.

The loaded cartridges can be ejected by the same process as that described for ejecting the empty shells ; should the *first* blow fail to eject the cartridge, it should be repeated.

CAUTION : Care must be taken to move the boss on the ring back to the *right* of the hammer after the ejection of the shells, so that the pistol will *always* be ready for firing except when the ejector is to be used.

There is a safety notch under the boss on the ring in rear of the cylinder, in which the hammer may rest when the pistol is not in use. The ring however, must be moved to the *right* in that case, so as to bring the firing-pin under the hammer, before the pistol can be fired.

The shells can be reloaded and used as often as may be required.

OFFICE OF COLT'S PAT. FIRE ARMS MFG. CO.
Hartford, Conn., 1868.

Directions accompanying Thuer Alteration sent to Gen. Dyer

Courtesy of The National Archives

alteration was designed for all models of the percussion Colt revolver currently being made, including the Root solid frame sidehammer. Adaptation to the latter is separately illustrated in the British patent drawings, and also described in the specifications. These call for a stationary ring in which a spring ejector may be released by a thumb piece so as to snap into each chamber as the cylinder is revolved. Except for the prototype in the Arthur L. Ulrich Museum, however, no example has come to the notice of the author.

Specimens of Thuer conversions of the .44 calibre 1860 Army and .36 calibre 1861 Navy are perhaps the most common, and are not infrequently found bearing British proofmarks. These are the only models quoted in the London price list of "Colt's New

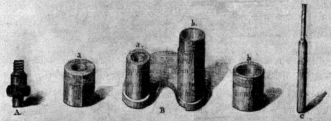

DIRECTIONS FOR RE-LOADING THE CARTRIDGES
FOR
COLTS METALLIC CARTRIDGE PISTOL.

Take off the cylinder.   Screw the plug A into the end of the rammer.   Then replace the barrel on the frame of the pistol, leaving the cylinder off.   Place the piece B so that its base will be where the rear of the cylinder was.

Having removed the exploded cap from the shell with the small end of the punch C, fit the shell over the stud *a*, place over the top of the shell the cap guide *a'* and drop a new cap into the hole in the cap guide *a'*.   Then bring the stud *a* under the rammer and push the cap into its place with the plug A, worked by the rammer.

Should the shell stick to the stud, it can be loosened by pushing it from the bottom with the large end of the punch C.

Having capped as many shells as may be required ; to finish the loading :

Remove the plug A from the rammer.   Drop the capped shell into the tube *b*, fill it with powder, and place a lubricant or a small lubricated wad above the powder.   Place the ball guide *b'* on insert in the top of *b'* the bullet, bring *b'* under the rammer, and push the bullet to its place with the rammer.

Should the cartridge stick in *b* or *b'*, it may be loosened with the large end of the punch C.

Reverse of 1869 London Price List

Patent Metallic Central Fire Cartridge Revolvers." While the charge for converting an old pistol was £1 17s. 6d., the price of a new Navy Thuer was the same, according to the 1869 London percussion price list, as that of a Navy cap and ball, and the Army Thuer was but five shillings more than its percussion predecessor. Metallic cartridges were quoted at one shilling to one and six more per hundred than paper ones.

Besides the 1860 and 1861 models, the author's collection contains specimens of Thuer alterations of the .31 calibre 1849 Pocket Model, the .36 calibre 1851 Navy and the .36 calibre 1862 Police Model. The cylinders of all specimens are chambered for six cartridges, which is uncommon in the case of the percussion 1849 Pocket Model and most unusual for the 1862. The 1849 Pocket, perhaps the rarest type of Thuer, is a dual-purpose specimen cased with an extra six-chambered percussion cylinder. With it the original serial numbers appear on the outside of the altered cylinder whereas with the 1862 specimen the cylinder is numbered differently than other parts. This cylinder may therefore have come from the hybrid model known as the "pocket pistol of navy calibre." The Thuer rings of both these specimens, which with the inside of their corresponding cylinders are specially numbered 75 and 5, are identical and interchangeable. They are stamped with the same inspector's mark, a small F. Other examples of small Thuers are known to the author with special serials 17 and 33 for the 1849 and 32 for the 1862.

The larger Thuer specimens in the author's collection—1851 Navy (two examples), 1860 Army and 1861 Navy—differ from the smaller models in that the thumb piece for turning the ring is at the top rather than on the left side of the cylinder, and is slotted so that the hammer may rest in it between the firing and ejecting positions. In the larger ring there is a stud which locks it in either position, whereas in the smaller it is held in the firing position by a spring. The larger specimens of ring are likewise identical and interchangeable, with much the same markings as the smaller type. Serial numbers on the outside of the altered cylinders correspond with those on other parts, while each ring and inside cylinder is separately numbered (respectively 174, 25, 12 and 7). There is an F on both 1851 Navys, the other models bear-

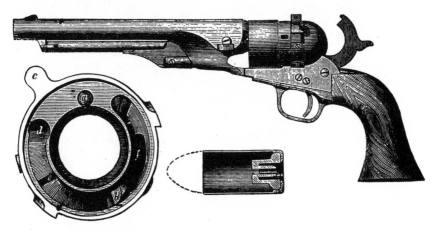

From the *Mechanics' Magazine,* July 23, 1869

ing British proofmarks but no inspector's stamp. Other examples of the 1860 Army and 1861 Navy are known to the author with special serials 10 and 42 in the first case and 13 in the latter.

It should be noted that all Thuers described up to this point are marked "PAT. SEP. 15, 1868" on the left side of the ring and have the script letter *&* over the ejecting lever. All but the 1862 model have had the end of the rammer drilled and threaded to take a reloading plug, and the 1849 and 1851 specimens have had their barrel frames cut out so that cartridges being loaded or ejected will clear. With the streamlined frames of the other models, this was not necessary. The patent specifications state that the chambers of the cylinder "may be tapering"—this is the case only in the above-mentioned 1860 Army and the 1862. Probably because of such reaming no fluted-cylinder alterations of these types are known. The author has heard of, but never seen, a Thuer conversion of the so-called 1853 Belt Model, and has examined several Dragoon Thuers of doubtful authenticity.

From the *United Services Gazette,* July 19, 1869

NOTES

FOREWORD

1. "The American Revolver and the West," *Scribner's Magazine,* Feb. 1927, Vol. 81, p. 127; see also Webb, *The Great
Plains* (1931), p. 167.

CHAPTER I: ANTECEDENT REVOLVERS

1. Purchase of Ordnance, House Exec. Doc. No. 99, 40th
Cong., 2nd Sess., January 14, 1868, pp. 100, 447, 730, 922,
Serial 1338. Compare Report of Chief of Ordnance, 1866,
p. 664, Serial 1285, giving total revolver purchases Jan. 1,
1861, to June 30, 1866.

2. Sale of Arms by U. S. Government, Senate Report No.
183, 42nd Cong., 2nd Sess., May 11, 1872, pp. 50, 62, 78,
Serial 1497.

3. Shannon, *The Organization and Administration of the
Union Army* (1928), Vol. I, pp. 69, 120; Official Records,
Series iii, Vol. 2, pp. 188, 191.

4. After the War Maj. Gen. Fitzhugh Lee, C.S.A., last Chief
of Cavalry in the Army of Northern Virginia, and General
Rosser, one of his division commanders, both named the
Colt revolver as the best arm for cavalry. See Denison,
*Modern Cavalry: Its Organization, Armament and Em-
ployment in War* (London, 1868), Appendices A and D,
pp. 351 and 368. Brig. Gen. Basil W. Duke, C.S.A., in
History of Morgan's Cavalry (1867), states at p. 178: "The
pistol preferred and usually worn by the men, was the
army Colt furnished to the Federal cavalry regiments."
See also *Memoirs of Colonel John S. Mosby* (1917), p. 285:
"I think we did more than any other body of men to give
the Colt pistol its great reputation."

5. "We had to have horses, and the United States Government unwillingly furnished us with at least one-third of our horses, saddles, bridles and carbines and Colts army pistols, and, last but not least, blankets and haversacks." U. R. Brooks, *Butler and His Cavalry in the War of Secession* (Columbia, S. C., 1909), p. 84. Maj. Gen. Matthew Calbraith Butler, C.S.A., of South Carolina, commanded a brigade and later a division in the Cavalry Corps of the Army of Northern Virginia.

A Canadian, Lt. Col. George T. Denison, Jr., wrote of the Colt in *Modern Cavalry: Its Organization, Armament and Employment in War* (1868), Appendix E, p. 374:

"The size adopted for the cavalry service during the late war in the Confederate States was what is called 'the army pistol.' The United States cavalry was furnished with this, and most of the Confederate cavalry supplied itself with the same arm, mainly by capture from their opponents."

6. *Army and Navy Journal*, Vol. 4, p. 474.

7. See James E. Serven's Catalog of the Albert Foster, Jr. Collection (1948), No. 342.

8. Cong. Globe Feb. 23, May 31 and June 22, 1870 (Pt. II, pp. 1500, 3949, 4695); Senate Exec. Doc. No. 23, 41st Cong., 2nd Sess., Serial 1405.

9. *Turf, Field and Farm*, Oct. 23, 1874, Vol. 19, p. 316.

10. *Army and Navy Journal*, Vol. 7, p. 85.

11. Report of the Secretary of War, 1867 (Report of Lt. Gen. Sherman, p. 32), Serial 1324; Grinnell, *The Fighting Cheyennes* (1915), p. 235; Wellman, *Death on Horseback* (1947), p. 52.

12. Ordnance Notes, No. CXV, Oct. 1, 1879, p. 163. Also found in Report of Chief of Ordnance, 1879, Appendix V, p. 315, Serial 1907. The absence of any revolvers taken at the Custer fight may be explained by an ordnance officer's observation that "every discussion regarding surrendered Indian arms proceeds on the assumption that the best have been cached." An Indian claim that they "obtained from Custer's command 592 carbines and revolvers" is noted in

Finerty, *War-Path and Bivouac* (1890), Appendix, p. 455. In 1878 Dull Knife's band of Northern Cheyennes still possessed "the Springfield carbines captured by them in the Custer fight" according to the Report of the Commissioner of Indian Affairs, 1878, p. xxiv. Also found in Report of the Secretary of the Interior, 1878, p. 457, Serial 1850.

13. Pp. 330, 340, Note 1, 365. None of the arms mentioned were taken at the Little Big Horn. The ease with which Indians could obtain breechloaders and metallic ammunition "outside the reservation" is noted in the Report of the Secretary of the Interior, 1879, pp. 14, 72, Serial 1910.

14. *Army and Navy Journal*, May 11, 1878, Vol. 15, p. 647.

15. His command of fifty scouts was armed with breechloading repeating Spencer rifles and Colt's percussion army revolvers. George A. Forsyth, *Thrilling Days in Army Life* (1900), pp. 11, 47.

16. *Army and Navy Journal*, Vol. 7, p. 768.

17. "The men were armed with the carbine and revolver; no one, not even the officer of the day, carried the sabre." Capt. Edward S. Godfrey, "Custer's Last Battle," *Century Magazine*, Jan., 1892, Vol. 53, p. 358. See also letter in the *Army and Navy Journal*, July 27, 1878, Vol. 15, p. 831, and Capt. Robert G. Carter, *On the Border with Mackenzie* (1935), p. 427. As early as 1865, Col. Albert G. Brackett wrote in his *History of the United States Cavalry*, p. 160: "The sabre in Indian fighting is simply a nuisance—they jingle abominably, and are of no earthly use."

CHAPTER II: EVOLUTION OF THE PEACEMAKER

1. Report of Chief of Ordnance, 1871, p. 252, Serial 1503.

2. Reports of Chief of Ordnance, 1872, 1873, Appendices C, p. 324 and B, p. 19, Class 8, Serials 1558, 1599.

3. Ordnance Notes, No. V, June 27, 1873, is the source of this and the following quotation.

4. Reports of Chief of Ordnance, 1873, p. 10, Serial 1599.

5. For initial advertisements see *Turf, Field and Farm*, Oct. 16 and 30, 1874, Vol. 19, pp. 292, 330. See also *Army and*

Navy Journal, May 13, 20 and 27, 1876, Vol. 13, pp. 638, 654 and 670, and editorial March 18, 1876, p. 514. The earliest advertisement known was in *The Illustrated London News,* Feb. 14, 1874, Vol. LXIV, p. 130: "Colt's New Government Pattern Army pistol takes the .450 Boxer Cartridge. It is the best pistol out."

6. Reports of Chief of Ordnance, 1874-1893, appendices on procurements and issues.

7. Frazier and Hunt, *I Fought with Custer* (1947), p. 92.

8. Testimony of Lieut. George G. Wallace at p. 10, Abstract of Record of Proceedings of a Court of Inquiry in the Case of Major Marcus A. Reno, Chicago, 1879 (ed. by Lt. Col. Wm. A. Graham, 1921); see also Capt. Edward S. Godfrey, "Custer's Last Battle," *Century Magazine,* Jan., 1892, Vol. 43, p. 358. Sergeant Windolph's recollection many years later was that each trooper had 24 rounds of revolver ammunition, but Lieut. Wallace testified to 18 soon after the event.

9. Grinnell, *The Fighting Cheyennes* (1915), p. 339.

10. Gen. Custer had already encountered Indians armed with breechloading repeating rifles in the Yellowstone Expedition of 1873. His report is quoted in Mulford, *Fighting Indians in the 7th United States Cavalry* (1879), p. 144.

11. Report of the Secretary of War, 1876 (Report of Gen. Crook, p. 500), Serial 1742. For a similar though less emphatic diary entry see *General George Crook, His Autobiography* (1946), p. 53. See also Col. Richard I. Dodge, *Our Wild Indians* (1882), p. 450.

CHAPTER III: THE SCHOFIELD SMITH & WESSON

1. Ordnance Notes, No. XXVII, July 27, 1874, is the source of this and two following quotations.

2. Reports of the Chief of Ordnance, 1874-1893, appendices on procurements and issues. The report for 1877 (Appendix A, Class VI, p. 18, Serial 1797) indicates that the second lot of Schofields procured was 5,000, not 3,000 as often stated. But inspection certificates for 3,000 only are to be found in the Springfield Armory files. Compare

McHenry and Roper, *Smith & Wesson Hand Guns* (1945), pp. 57, 219; Gluckman, *United States Martial Pistols & Revolvers* (1939), p. 235; Satterlee, *A Catalog of Firearms for the Collector* (1927), p. 145.

3. Records of the War Dept., U. S. Army Commands, File 5212 D. D. 1877, The National Archives.

4. Sept. 30, 1877, in northern Montana. *Personal Recollections of General Nelson A. Miles* (1896), p. 272; Howard and McGrath, *War Chief Joseph* (1941), p. 271. Capt. Edward S. Godfrey, 7th Cavalry, was awarded the Congressional Medal of Honor for leading his troop in this fight after he was wounded.

5. *Turf, Field and Farm,* Sept. 14, 1877, Vol. 25, p. 174; *Army and Navy Journal,* Sept. 29, 1877, Vol. 15, p. 13.

6. *Army and Navy Journal,* March 31, 1877, Vol. 14, p. 562.

7. *December* 19, 1882, p. 4; see also *Army and Navy Journal,* December 23, 1882, Vol. 20, p. 461.

CHAPTER IV: THE REMINGTON MODEL OF 1875

1. *Army and Navy Journal,* Vol. 14, p. 435.

2. See for example Karr, *Remington Handguns* (1947), pp. 62, 124; Gluckman, *United States Martial Pistols & Revolvers* (1939), p. 230; Satterlee, *A Catalog of Firearms for the Collector* (1927), p. 112.

3. Correspondence from Baron Von Oppen in the Ulrich Museum indicates that this order was placed after an offer by Gen. Effatoun Pasha of Cairo to purchase 10,000 Single Action Army revolvers at £2 per pistol was rejected by Colt's.

4. Report of April 28, 1877. The National Archives, Records of the War Department, Office of the Chief of Ordnance, Springfield Armory Reports, 1874-1878.

5. Pp. 174-214, Plates XXX and XXXI.

CHAPTER V: CONTEMPORARY OPINIONS

1. See Chap. II, Note 5.

2. *Army and Navy Journal,* May 6, 1876, Vol. 13, p. 630.

3. *Army and Navy Journal,* Vol. 14, p. 566.

4. *Army and Navy Journal,* Vol. 14, p. 594.
5. *Army and Navy Journal,* Vol. 14, p. 675.
6. These letters are reported in the *Army and Navy Journal* of April 13, 1878, Vol. 15, p. 569.
7. Report of Chief of Ordnance, 1877, Appendix L (Report of Lt. Col. Benton, p. 572 and Fig. 102), Serial 1797.
8. *Army and Navy Journal,* Vol. 15, p. 662.
9. United States Centennial Commission, International Exhibition, Philadelphia, 1876, Vol. 6, pp. 29, 61 (Group XVI, Class 265).
10. Report of Chief of Ordnance, 1876, Appendix F (Report of Lieut. Metcalfe, p. 35), Serial 1746.
11. *Hunting Trips of a Ranchman* (1885), pp. 13, 39. For contemporaneous illustrations by Frederic Remington of life in the cow country, see Roosevelt, *Ranch Life and the Hunting Trail* (1888), *passim.*
12. Vol. 63, p. 58 (Jan. 12, 1884), p. 158 (Feb. 2), p. 512 (April 12), p. 530 (April 19). See also Major H. E. C. Kitchener, "Revolvers and Their Use," *R.U.S.I. Journal,* July 14, 1886, Vol. XXX, pp. 951, 968.
13. Vol. 64, p. 549 (Oct. 18, 1884).
14. *The Modern Sportsman's Gun and Rifle* (1884), Vol. II, pp. 419, 421. Walsh did not discriminate between Colt's single and double actions.

CHAPTER VI: MULTIBALL CARTRIDGES

1. Report of Chief of Ordnance, 1879, Appendix W, pp. 329 *et seq.* (Serial 1907) is the source of this chapter and of the quotations not otherwise identified.
2. Report of Chief of Ordnance, 1879, p. 19, Serial 1907.
3. *Army and Navy Journal,* August 9, 1879, Vol. 17, p. 10.
4. Reports of Chief of Ordnance, 1879, 1880, Appendices B, p. 33, and 2, p. 11, Class VIII, Serials 1907, 1956.
5. "Sabers or Revolvers?", *Cavalry Journal,* March, 1888, Vol. I, pp. 38, 50.
6. See Chap. VIII, Note 11.

Lieut. Swift's views were echoed by other Cavalry officers in the *Military Service Institution Journal,* Vol. XIV

(1893). Col. A. K. Arnold, 1st Cavalry, said at p. 101: "A pistol for *close work* . . . should be chambered for four rounds, the calibre being about that of a 12 gauge shotgun . . . each chamber carrying four balls." Lieut. William H. Smith, 10th Cavalry, said at p. 110: "My idea of a cavalry pistol is to have a five-inch barrel, five chambered fifty-five calibre pistol carrying a round ball and three buckshot." Lieut. Powhatan H. Clarke, 9th Cavalry, said at p. 113: "I have used two gallery bullets and a diminished charge in the Colt cal. 45 with excellent results at 20 paces . . . A pistol the chamber of which would hold three of these round cal. 45 balls would suit my idea."

CHAPTER VII: OTHER RIVALS

1. Records of the War Dept., Office of the Chief of Ordnance, Springfield Armory Reports, Dec. 8, 1874-Jan. 4, 1875, The National Archives.
2. Sept. 2, 1882, Vol. 20, p. 110, and weekly thereafter until Nov. 25th.

CHAPTER VIII: ADOPTION OF THE DOUBLE ACTION

1. Endorsement of August 10, 1878. The National Archives, Records of the War Department, Office of the Chief of Ordnance, Springfield Armory, Letters Sent, June, 1876-October, 1879.
2. See Col. J. C. Kelton, "The Kelton Devices," *Cavalry Journal,* March, 1888, Vol. I, pp. 60, 65; U. S. Patent No. 333,416 of Dec. 29, 1885; Records of the War Dept., Office of the Chief of Ordnance, File 3214 (1886), The National Archives. See also Report of Chief of Ordnance, 1887, p. 5, Serial 2538.
3. Report of Secretary of Navy, 1887 (Report of Chief of Bureau of Ordnance, p. 234), Serial 2539.
4. Reports of Secretary of Navy, 1888, 1889 (Reports of Chief of Bureau of Ordnance, pp. 188, 441), Serials 2634, 2721; *Journal of Franklin Institute,* May, 1890, Vol. CXXIX, p. 405.

5. Report of Chief of Ordnance, 1889, Appendix 12, p. 129, Serial 2720.

6. Capt. Richard A. Williams, 8th Cavalry, "On Pistol Firing," *Cavalry Journal,* Dec. 1889, Vol. II, pp. 337, 342.

7. "Revolver Shooting," *Cavalry Journal,* March, 1889, Vol. II, pp. 37, 38.

8. *Army and Navy Journal,* April 5, 1890, Vol. 27, p. 601.

9. Report of Chief of Ordnance, 1891, p. 25, Serial 2928.

10. This preference was shared by Lieut. Powhatan H. Clarke, 10th Cavalry, whose views are noted in *The Cavalry Journal* of June, 1890, Vol. III, p. 222.

11. This view was shared, if not expressed in the report, by Lieut. Eben Swift, 5th Cavalry, who deplored the reduction of calibre in an article entitled "The New Revolver," *Cavalry Journal,* March, 1893, Vol. VI, p. 84. He cited experiences of British officers in savage warfare in Africa and India, from Major H. E. C. Kitchener's "Revolvers and Their Use," *R.U.S.I. Journal,* July 14, 1886, Vol. XXX, pp. 951, 970. See also Lieut. James A. Cole, 6th Cavalry, "Queries on the Cavalry Equipment," *Military Service Institution Journal,* Vol. XIII, pp. 1076, 1078 (1892).

12. Report of Chief of Ordnance, 1892, Appendix 15, p. 341, Serial 3083; *Army and Navy Journal,* April 16, 1892, Vol. 29, p. 597.

13. Report of Chief of Ordnance, 1892, p. 31, Serial 3083.

14. Report of Chief of Ordnance, 1893, p. 203, Appendices 2, p. 67, and 3, p. 91, Class VI, Serial 3205.

15. "On Pistols," *R.U.S.I. Journal,* Dec., 1896, Vol. XL, p. 1460.

16. O'Byrne, *The Victoria Cross* (1880), p. 151; Sir John Miller Adye, "The Umbeyla Campaign of 1863," *Journal of the Society for Army Historical Research* (1940), Vol. 19, No. 73, p. 43.

17. "The Caliber of the Revolver," *Journal of the Military Service Institution,* March, 1905, Vol. XXXVI, pp. 300, 301.

CHAPTER IX: POPULARITY OF THE MODEL "P"

1. For initial advertisement by John P. Moore's Sons, see *Army and Navy Journal*, Feb. 2, 1878, Vol. 15, p. 402. Production began in 1877.

2. *Sam¹ Colt's Own Record of Transactions with Walker and Whitney in 1847* (Conn. Hist. Soc., 1949), p. 65.

3. See Ramon F. Adams, *Western Words* (1944), *passim*.

4. See Briggs, *Frontiers of the Northwest* (1940), pp. 274, 293.

5. Heitman, *Historical Register and Dictionary of the United States Army* (1903).

6. Viz., advertisement of B. Kittredge & Co., Oct. 13, 1877, Vol. 15, p. 146.

7. Thompson, "Bat Masterson; The Dodge City Years," Fort Hays Kansas State College Bulletin, 1943, Vol. XXXII, No. 18.

8. This was the nom de plume of Edward Zane Carroll Judson, 1823-1886. Pond, *Life and Adventures of Ned Buntline* (1919).

9. Burr, *Four Thousand Years of World's Progress* (Hartford, 1878), p. 97.

10. For a photograph of Captain Jack with his Peacemaker stuck in his belt, see Schmitt and Brown, *Fighting Indians of the West* (1949), p. 171.

11. Crawford, *The Poet Scout* (1879), p. 68. Smith, *A Famous Battery and Its Campaigns, 1861-4* (1892), p. 156.

12. Miguel A. Otero, *My Life on the Frontier* (1935), Vol. I, p. 18.

13. *Forty Years on the Frontier* (1925), Vol. II, pp. 183, 193, 201.

14. Cooper, *Stirring Lives of Buffalo Bill and Pawnee Bill* (1912), *passim*.

CHAPTER X: VARIATIONS AND TARGET TYPES

1. See *Turf, Field and Farm*, Oct. 23, 1874, Vol. 19, p. 316.

2. March 9, 1895, Vol. CVI, p. 309, and every two weeks thereafter until June 29th.

3. Capt. A. H. East, Hampshire Regiment, in *R.U.S.I. Journal*, Dec., 1896, Vol. XL, p. 1479.
4. The Peacemaker was tested in 1874 by the Military School of Musketry at Spandau, Prussia, against Smith & Wesson and Pirlot (Belgian) revolvers. Single actions chambered for a .44 centerfire cartridge were furnished for this trial.
5. Col. Robert S. Allen, *Lucky Forward* (1947), p. 44, and photographs, pp. 82, 274; see also frontispiece, Patton, *War as I Knew It* (1947).

CHAPTER XI: SERIAL NUMBERS AND SALES

1. Order of Jan. 31, 1871, Gen. A. B. Dyer to Gen. W. B. Franklin. The National Archives, Records of the War Department, Office of the Chief of Ordnance, Miscellaneous Letters Sent, Volume 71. "500 Army Revolvers altered to B/L" were shipped from Colt's to the Springfield Armory August 18, 1871. Letter Colt's to Col. J. G. Benton, *ibid.*, Miscellaneous Letters Received, 1871, No. 452.

CHAPTER XIII: PATENTS AND PIRATES

1. No. 117,461. Charles B. Richards, later professor of mechanical engineering at Yale, was then assistant superintendent of the Colt factory.
2. Nos. 123,644 and 158,957.
3. Assignment recorded July 31, 1874, in U. S. Patent Office.
4. British Patent Oct. 22, 1867, No. 2961; U. S. Patent Dec. 29, 1868, No. 85,350.
5. See William Mason's specifications of Jan. 19, 1875. A Richards conversion with an infringing gate is illustrated in Parsons, *Catalog of a Loan Exhibition of Percussion Colt Revolvers and Conversions, 1836-1873* (Metropolitan Museum of Art, 1942), Plate XXXIX, No. 121.
6. In letter of January 23, 1950, The National Archives reported finding in its files "no information relating to the manufacture of a miniature, single action .38 calibre Colt revolver at the Springfield Armory."

CHAPTER XIV: SIGNIFICANCE OF THE REVOLVER

1. Walter Prescott Webb, "The American Revolver and the West," *Scribner's Magazine*, Feb., 1927, Vol. 81, p. 178.

2. Parsons, "Samuel Colt's Medals from the American Institute," *New-York Historical Society Quarterly*, July, 1949, Vol. XXXIII, p. 198.

3. See R. W. G. Vail, *Gold Fever, A Catalogue of the California Gold Rush Centennial Exhibition* (New-York Hist. Soc., 1949), pp. 31, 32 and 40.

4. The author of *A Journey Through Texas, or, A Saddle-Trip on the Southwestern Frontier* armed himself and two companions with a Sharps rifle, a double fowling piece, Colt's Navy revolvers, and sheathed hunting knives. His full comment on the revolvers, which their inventor might well have used for advertising copy, but apparently overlooked, read at p. 75:

   "Of the Colt's we cannot speak in too high terms. Though subjected for six or eight months to rough use, exposed to damp grass, and to all the ordinary neglects and accidents of camp travel, not once did a ball fail to answer the finger. Nothing got out of order, nothing required care; not once though carried at random, in coat-pocket or belt, or tied thumping at the pummel, was there an accidental discharge. In short, they simply gave us perfect satisfaction, being all they claimed to be. Before taking them from home we gave them a trial alongside every rival we could hear of, and we had with us an unpatented imitation, but for practical purposes one Colt we found worth a dozen of all others. Such was the testimony of every old hunter and ranger we met. There are probably in Texas about as many revolvers as male adults, and I doubt if there are one hundred in the state of any other make."

5. Col. R. B. Marcy, *Thirty Years of Army Life on the Border* (1866), p. 287; Stuart, *Forty Years on the Frontier* (1925), Vol. I, p. 122.

6. Parsons, "The Colt Brevete," *American Rifleman*, June, 1950, Vol. 98, p. 22.

7. Major G. Tylden, "The Use of Fire Arms by Cavalry," *Journal of the Society for Army Historical Research* (1940), Vol. 19, No. 73, pp. 9, 11; Kinglake, *The Invasion of the Crimea* (1888), Vol. II, pp. 533, 535 and 563; Forbes, *Camps, Quarters and Casual Places* (1896), p. 86.

8. The opinions of Maj. Gen. Fitzhugh Lee and Lt. Gen. Stephen D. Lee, C.S.A., are quoted by Lt. Col. Denison in *Modern Cavalry: Its Organization, Armament and Employment in War* (London, 1868), Appendices A and C, pp. 351 and 362. For a later contrary view see Bvt. Maj. Gen. Wesley Merritt, U.S.A., in "Cavalry: Its Organization and Armament," *Military Service Institution Journal*, Vol. I, pp. 42, 45 (1879). Lt. Col. Denison, who inclined to the Confederate view, commented in his book at p. 59:

"There is no doubt that the revolver is beyond all odds the best pistol for mounted forces of any description. Colt's revolver is a splendid weapon, but it should be loaded with detonating cartridges so as to save the capping. There is a modification of this pistol, which is loaded by taking the cylinder out and dropping the six cartridges from the rear into the chambers, and then the cylinder is returned to its place and fastened in."

His last sentence is the earliest mention found of the rear-loading field alteration of the Colt, antedating the Thuer and Richards conversions.

9. Maj. Gen. James H. Wilson, U.S.V., Chief of Cavalry in the Military Division of the Mississippi, describes the Spencer carbine as "the most effective fire arm of the day" in *Under the Old Flag* (1912), Vol. I, pp. 331, 374.

10. See remarks of Benjamin F. Butler in House of Representatives, Cong. Globe, June 22, 1870, 41st Cong., 2nd Sess. (Pt. V, p. 4696).

11. See Appendix, p. 154.

12. Capt. Geo. Vidmer, 11th Cavalry, in "The Service Pistol," *Cavalry Journal*, Oct., 1905, Vol. XVI, states at p. 185:

"From 1873 to 1894 our army's experience was obtained in Indian warfare, where the pistol played a minor part.

It was true that it was used, and by some regiments to more or less extent, but never to such an extent that justifies comparing these times with those in the Civil War. It was in the Civil War that the pistol developed itself, proved its efficiency and necessity, and made for itself a place in the armament of our cavalrymen."

13. Sheriff Pat F. Garrett states Billy carried a "self-cocker, calibre .41" in *The Authentic Life of Billy, the Kid* (1882), p. 129.

14. See Chap. V, Note 11.

15. Cushman, "Abilene, First of the Kansas Cow Towns," *Kansas Historical Quarterly,* August, 1940, Vol. IX, p. 250; Lake, *Wyatt Earp, Frontier Marshal* (1931), p. 140. For a fatal incident in Las Vegas, N. M. see Otero, *My Life on the Frontier* (1935), Vol. I, p. 186.

16. Nordyke, *Cattle Empire* (1949), Appendix, p. 264. Compare resolution of the Wyoming Stock Growers Association in 1882:

"Whereas the custom of carrying fire arms by those engaged in the round-up and in working the cattle ranges is productive of great evil and frequently results in the damage of persons and property. Be it therefore *Resolved,* That the custom of carrying fire arms, except in the immediate vicinity of Indian reservations, should be discontinued. . . ."

Spring, *Seventy Years, a panoramic history of the Wyoming Stock Growers Association* (Cheyenne, 1942), p. 31.

17. Emerson Hough, in *The Story of the Cowboy* (1897), notes at p. 58:

"The wearing of arms upon the person is in many of the western territories now prohibited by law, and it is no longer customary to see the cowpuncher wearing the revolver or even carrying the Winchester which at a time not many years ago were part of his regular outfit."

18. The prevalence of six-shooters in the Alaskan gold fields is attested in Walden, *A Dog-Puncher on the Yukon* (1928), pp. 147, 165, 264 and Adney, *The Klondike Stampede* (1900), p. 426.

APPENDIX: THE THUER CONVERSION

1. U. S. Patent April 3, 1855, No. 12,648.
2. *White v. Allen* and *White v. Boker,* 29 Fed. Cas. 969 (Dist. Ct. Mass. 1863) and 981 (Dist. Ct. N. Y. 1862). The decree of the Federal District Court of Massachusetts was affirmed Feb. 8, 1869, by a tie vote of the U. S. Supreme Court.
3. Parsons, *Catalogue of a Loan Exhibition of Percussion Colt Revolvers and Conversions, 1836-1873,* published by The Metropolitan Museum of Art (New York, 1942), p. 33.
4. U. S. Patent April 13, 1858, No. 19,961.
5. British Patent June 1, 1867, No. 1625; see also U. S. Patent Oct. 3, 1865, No. 50,224.
6. U. S. Patent Sept. 20, 1864, No. 44,363, assignment recorded Dec. 26, 1867.
7. U. S. Patent April 7, 1866, No. 53,955.
8. '69 C. D. 107.
9. Oct. 22, 1869. See also W. W. Greener, *Modern Breech-Loaders* (London, 1871), p. 156.
10. Senate Exec. Doc. 23, 41st Cong. 2nd Sess. Vol. 1, Serial 1405; House Report 84, 42nd Cong. 3rd Sess. Vol. 1, Serial 1576.
11. U. S. Patent No. 117,461. A supplementary patent on an improved ejecting rod was taken by Wm. Mason July 2, 1872, No. 123,644.

BIBLIOGRAPHY

PERIODICALS

American Rifleman. Washington, 1949-1950.
Army and Navy Journal. New York, 1867-1893.
Cavalry Journal. Washington, 1888-1906.
Century Magazine. New York, 1888-1892.
The Engineer. London, 1869.
The Field. London, 1874-1884.
Franklin Institute Journal. Philadelphia, 1890.
Illustrated London News. London, 1867-1895.
Kansas Historical Quarterly. Topeka, 1940.
Mechanics' Magazine. London, 1869.
Military Service Institution Journal. New York, 1879-1905.
New-York Historical Society Quarterly. New York, 1949.
Royal United Service Institution Journal. London, 1886-1896.
Scribner's Magazine. New York, 1927.
Society for Army Historical Research Journal. London, 1940.
Turf, Field and Farm. New York, 1874-1878.
United Services Gazette. London, 1869.

PAMPHLETS

Burr, Samuel J., and S. DeVere, *Four Thousand Years of World's Progress.* Hartford, 1878.
Graham, Lt. Col. Wm. A. (ed.), *Abstract of Record of Proceedings of a Court of Inquiry in Case of Major Marcus A. Reno, 7th Cavalry. Chicago, 1879.* Washington, 1921.
Parsons, John E., *Catalogue of a Loan Exhibition of Percussion Colt Revolvers and Conversions, 1836-1873.* Metropolitan Museum of Art, New York, 1942.

173

Serven, James E., *Catalog of Albert Foster, Jr. Collection*. Santa Ana, Calif., 1948.
Spring, Agnes Wright, *Seventy Years, a panoramic history of the Wyoming Stock Growers Association*. Cheyenne, 1942.
Thompson, George G., *Bat Masterson; The Dodge City Years*. Kansas State College, Topeka, 1943.
Vail, R. W. G., *Gold Fever, A Catalogue of the California Gold Rush Centennial Exhibition*. New-York Historical Society, 1949.

GOVERNMENT REPORTS

Chief of Ordnance (U. S. Army), Annual Reports, 1866-1895.
Chief of the Bureau of Ordnance (U. S. Navy), Annual Reports, 1887-9.
Commissioner of Indian Affairs, Annual Reports, 1871-9.
Congressional Globe, 1870.
House Executive Document No. 99, 40th Cong., 2nd Sess., 1868.
House Report No. 84, 42nd Cong., 3rd Sess., 1873.
Official Records, War of the Rebellion, Series III, Vol. 2.
Ordnance Memoranda, Nos. 9, 11, 22, 29.
Ordnance Notes, Nos. V, XXVII, LIV, LXXVI, CXV.
Patent Office Specifications and Drawings.
Secretary of the Interior, Annual Reports, 1871-9.
Secretary of the Navy, Annual Reports, 1887-9.
Secretary of War, Annual Reports, 1866-1895.
Senate Executive Document No. 23, 41st Cong., 2nd Sess., 1870.
Senate Report No. 183, 42nd Cong., 2nd Sess., 1872.
U. S. Centennial Commission, International Exhibition, Philadelphia, 1876, Report, Vol. 6.

MILITARY MEMOIRS

Allen, Col. Robert S., *Lucky Forward, the history of Patton's Third U. S. Army*. New York, 1947.
Bourke, Capt. John G., *On the Border with Crook*. New York, 1891.
Brackett, Col. Albert G., *History of the United States Cavalry to June 1, 1863*. New York, 1865.

Brooks, U. R., *Butler and His Cavalry in the War of Secession.* Columbia, S. C., 1909.

Carter, Capt. Robert G., *On the Border with Mackenzie; or Winning West Texas from the Comanches.* Washington, 1935.

Crook, Maj. Gen. George, *General George Crook, His Autobiography.* Norman, Okla., 1946.

Denison, Lt. Col. George T., Jr., *Modern Cavalry; Its Organization, Armament and Employment in War.* Toronto, 1868.

Duke, Brig. Gen. Basil W., *History of Morgan's Cavalry.* Cincinnati, 1867.

Forbes, Archibald, *Camps, Quarters and Casual Places.* London, 1896.

Forsyth, Brig. Gen. George A., *Thrilling Days in Army Life.* New York, 1900.

Finerty, John F., *War-Path and Bivouac; or, The Conquest of the Sioux.* Chicago, 1890.

Gilmor, Col. Harry, *Four Years in the Saddle.* New York, 1866.

Heitman, Francis B., *Historical Register and Dictionary of the United States Army.* 2 vols. Government Printing Office, Washington, 1903.

Hunt, Frazier and Robert, *I Fought with Custer: The Story of Sergeant Windolph.* New York, 1947.

Kinglake, Alexander Wm., *The Invasion of the Crimea.* 6 vols. New York, 1863-1888.

Marcy, Col. Randolph Barnes, *Thirty Years of Army Life on the Border.* New York, 1866.

Mosby, Col. John S., *Memoirs of Colonel John S. Mosby.* Boston, 1917.

Miles, Lt. Gen. Nelson A., *Personal Recollections and Observations of General Nelson A. Miles.* Chicago, 1897.

Mulford, Ami Frank, *Fighting Indians in the 7th United States Cavalry.* Corning, N. Y., 1879.

O'Byrne, Robert W., *The Victoria Cross.* London, 1880.

Patton, Gen. George S., Jr., *War as I Knew It.* Boston, 1947.

Shannon, Fred A., *The Organization and Administration of the Union Army.* 2 vols. Cleveland, 1928.

Smith, James E., *A Famous Battery and Its Campaigns, 1861-'64.*
Washington, 1892.
Wilson, Maj. Gen. James H., *Under the Old Flag.* 2 vols. New
York, 1912.

WESTERN AMERICANA

Adams, Ramon F., *Western Words: a Dictionary of the Range,
Cow Camp and Trail.* Norman, Okla., 1944.
Adney, Tappan, *The Klondike Stampede.* New York, 1900.
Armstrong, Maj. Neville A. D., *Yukon Yesterdays.* London,
1936.
Briggs, Harold E., *Frontiers of the Northwest.* New York, 1940.
Cook, James H., *Fifty Years on the Old Frontier.* New Haven,
1923.
Cooper, Frank C., *Stirring Lives of Buffalo Bill and Pawnee
Bill.* New York, 1912.
Cox, James, *The Cattle Industry of Texas and Adjacent Ter-
ritory.* St. Louis, 1895.
Crawford, John Wallace, *The Poet Scout.* San Francisco, 1879.
Dodge, Col. Richard I., *Our Wild Indians.* Hartford, 1882.
Garrett, Pat F., *The Authentic Life of Billy, the Kid.* Santa
Fe, 1882.
Grinnell, George Bird, *The Fighting Cheyennes.* New York,
1915.
Hough, Emerson, *The Story of the Cowboy.* New York, 1897.
Howard, Helen A., and McGrath, Dan L., *War Chief Joseph.*
Caldwell, Idaho, 1941.
Lake, Stuart A., *Wyatt Earp, Frontier Marshal.* Boston, 1931.
Nordyke, Lewis, *Cattle Empire.* New York, 1949.
Olmsted, Frederick Law, *A Journey through Texas, or a Saddle
Trip on the Southwestern Frontier.* New York, 1857.
Otero, Miguel A., *My Life on the Frontier.* 2 vols. New York,
1935-1939.
Pond, Frederick E., *Life and Adventures of "Ned Buntline."*
New York, 1919.
Roosevelt, Col. Theodore, *Hunting Trips of a Ranchman.* New
York, 1885.

Roosevelt, Col. Theodore, *Ranch Life and the Hunting-Trail.*
New York, 1888.

Schmitt, Martin F., and Brown, Dee, *Fighting Indians of the
West.* New York, 1948.

Stuart, Granville, *Forty Years on the Frontier.* 2 vols. Cleveland, 1925.

Vestal, Stanley, *War Path and Council Fire.* New York, 1948.

Walden, Arthur T., *A Dog Puncher on the Yukon.* Boston,
1928.

Webb, Walter Prescott, *The Great Plains.* Boston, 1931.

Wellman, Paul I., *Death on Horseback.* Philadelphia, 1947.

FIREARMS BOOKS

Benton, Lt. Col. James G., *Fabrication of Small Arms for
United States Service.* Government Printing Office, Washington, 1878.

Deyrup, Felicia J., *Arms Makers of the Connecticut Valley.*
Northampton, Mass., 1948.

Gluckman, Maj. Arcadi, *United States Martial Pistols.* Buffalo,
1939.

Gould, A. C., *Modern American Pistols & Revolvers.* Boston,
1888.

Greener, W. W., *Modern Breech-Loaders.* London, 1871.

Haven, Charles T., and Belden, Frank A., *A History of the
Colt Revolver.* New York, 1940.

Karr, Charles L. and Caroll R., *Remington Hand Guns.* Har-
risburg, 1947.

McHenry, Roy C., and Roper, Walter F., *Smith & Wesson
Hand Guns.* Huntington, West Virginia, 1945.

Norton, Brig. Gen. Charles B., *American Breech Loading Small
Arms.* New York, 1872.

Parsons, John E. (ed.), *Sam¹ Colt's Own Record of Transactions
with Captain Walker and Eli Whitney, Jr. in 1847.* Connecticut Historical Society, 1949.

Satterlee, *A Catalog of Fire Arms for the Collector.* Detroit,
1927.

Walsh, John Henry, *The Modern Sportsman's Gun and Rifle.*
2 vols. London, 1884.

INDEX

Abercrombie & Fitch, of New York, 118
Adams, John, British patentee, 130
Adams revolver, 8, 55, 137, 150, 152
Abilene, Kansas, 140
Alaska Juneau, G. M. Co., 95
Allen, Ethan, of Worcester, firearms manufacturer, 64
American Express Co., employees armed with Schofield, 35
Ammunition, Bridgeport, 38, 40, 47
Anaconda Copper Mining Co., 95
Anderson, A. J., of Ft. Worth, firearms dealer, 115
Apache Indians, 91
Arikaree River, 15
Arizona Copper Co., 95
Army Model of 1860, 5, 6, 8, 19, 111; converted, 10, 18, 19, 112, 128, 170
Army Model of 1872, tested, 13, 20; serial numbers, 112
Army Model of 1873, tested, 18, 20; selected, 21; procurements and issues, 23; refinished, 26; survival rate, 27; tested against Schofield and Remington, 36; rusting test, 38; dimensions, weight and firing, 38; endurance and fouling, 39; diagrams, 40, 42, 43; preferred to others, 40; stamping, 44, 102; editorial comment, 46; exhibited at Philadelphia, 52; rejected by War Office, 55; altered for multiball, 56, 57; tested against Forehand & Wadsworth, 64; compared to Merwin Hulbert, 71; adopted by 7th Cavalry, 24, 73; criticized, 77; shipped to Philippines, 26, 83
Arnold, Col. A. K., 1st Cavalry, quoted, 165
Ashdown, J. H., Hardware Co., of Winnipeg, 118
Avriet, Giles C., of Cameron, Texas, 95

Babcock & Miles, of Billings, Montana, firearms dealer, 116
Baker & Hamilton, of San Francisco, firearms dealer, 118
Barrel lengths, 96, 102, 108
Beaumont, Texas, police, 119
Belknap, W. B., & Co. of Louisville, firearms dealer, 116
Benét, Gen. Steven Vincent, Chief of Ordnance, 28; quoted, 58
Bennett, T. G., of Winchester's, 132
Benton, Col. James G., Commandant of Springfield Armory, 28, 64; monograph on small arms, 44; quoted, 57, 73
Bering-Cortes Hardware Co., of Houston, 116
Bernie, Lieut. Rogers, of Ordnance Dept., 59, 61
Bettes, H. S., of Paris, Texas, firearms dealer, 118
Billy the Kid, 139, 170
Bisley Models, 104-108; calibres, 122, 124
Blish, Mize & Silliman, of Atchison, Kansas, firearms dealer, 118
Blount, Capt. S. E., of Ordnance Dept., 79
Boker, Herman, & Co., of New York, firearms dealer, 115
Bonebrake Hardware & Implement Co.. of El Reno, Oklahoma, 118
Bowie knife, 135
Boxer cartridge, 106, 150, 162
Britain, Battle of, 3, 120
British Purchasing Commission, 120
Browning Brothers, of Ogden, Utah, firearms dealer, 116
Buffalo Bill, 97, 99
Bullard, Maj. Robert Lee, on fighting Moros, 82
Buntline Special, 48, 96

178

Burkhard, William R., of St. Paul, firearms dealer, 115
Butler, Gen. Mathew C., Confederate
cavalryman, 160

Calibres, 42, 84, 100, 103, 106, 108, 110,
111, 121, 124; tables, 126-127
Cananea Consol. Copper Co., of Sonora,
95
Cardigan, Lord, 137
Carr, Capt. C. C. C., 1st Cavalry, 75
Catlin, George, 137
Cavalry, equipment of, 12, 16, 23, 34,
47, 50, 52, 75, 78, 137, 159, 160
Charge of the Light Brigade, 137
Cheyenne Indians, 3, 13, 14, 139, 160
China-Japan Trading Co., 95
Churchill, Winston, quoted, 120
Civil War, 5, 7, 52, 76, 88, 137, 170
Clarke, Lieut. Powhatan, H., 9th Cav-
alry, quoted, 165
Cody, Col. William F., 85, 99
Coeur d'Alene Hardware Co., of Wal-
lace, Idaho, 118
Cole, Lieut. James A., 6th Cavalry, 166
Colt Allies, 115
Colt-Burgess rifle, 132
Colt revolvers, see various models
Colt, Samuel, nickname, 84
Colt's Manufacturing Co., 32, 81, 115,
143
Comanche Indians, 91
Combaluzier, A., of Mexico City, fire-
arms dealer, 116
Confederate Army, percussion Colt in,
7, 137, 159, 160
Copper Queen Consol. Mining Co., 95
Cornelius, Ed., of Erath County, Texas,
95
Cowboys and frontiersmen, preference,
3, 53, 54, 139
Crawford, Capt. Jack, verse quoted, 97
Crook, Gen. George, on Indian fight-
ing, 24
Crook, J. B., & Co., of New York, fire-
arms dealer, 118
Crowell, George C., patentee, 144
Crimean War, 137
Crispin, Silas, patentee, 144
Curry, N., & Bro., of San Francisco,
firearms dealer, 115
Custer's last stand, 13, 14, 24; arms cap-
tured, 160

Dakota, Department of, 33, 73; Terri-
tory, 53
Deadwood, S. D., 98
Deane revolver, 158
Denison, Lt. Col. George T., quoted
on revolver, 160, 170
Departamento de Consignaciones, 95
Deutz, A., & Bros., of Laredo, firearms
dealer, 118
Dixon, Col., of War Office, examines
Thuer, 148
Dodge City, Kansas, 91, 96, 140
Dodge, W. C., of Washington, 58
Double Action .38 of 1877, 34, 139
Double Action .45 of 1878, criticized,
73; advertised, 74; "Alaskan Model,"
83; discontinued, 105
Double Action .38 of 1889, tested, 76,
78; preferred to Smith & Wesson, 79;
compared to .45, 79; adopted, 80;
stopping power, 63, 82
Dragoon Model, 5
Drew, Reuben W., patentee, 129
Duke, Gen. Basil W., on use of Colt
by Morgan's Cavalry, 160
Dunham, Carrigan & Hayden Co., of
San Francisco, firearms dealer, 118
Dyer, Gen. A. B., Chief of Ordnance,
16, 153

Eadie, Capt. John R., of Ordnance
Dept., quoted, 18, 28
Earp, Wyatt, 91, 96
Effatoun Pasha, Gen., of Cairo, 163
Eibar, 134
El Paso Saddlery Co., firearms dealer,
116
Emery, C. A., draughtsman at Spring-
field Armory, 36
Enfield, Royal Small Arms Factory at,
55

Farley, Capt. J. P., of Ordnance Dept.,
32, 36, 64
Farnsworth, C. A., of Grant County,
N. M., 95
Farwell-Ozmun, Kirk & Co., of St. Paul,
firearms dealer, 116
Fetterman Massacre, 13
Finishes, 103
Flagler, Gen. D. W., Chief of Ordnance,
quoted, 80
Folsom, H. & D., of New York, fire-
arms dealer, 115

Forehand, Sullivan, of Worcester, firearms manufacturer, 66
Forehand & Wadsworth revolver, 64; dimensions, 65; tested against Colt, 66; illustrated, 67
Forsyth, Col. George A., stand at Arikaree River, 15, 161
Fort Phil Kearney, Wyoming, 13
Fosbery, Lt. Col. G. W., on stopping power, 81
Frankfort Arsenal, 56
Franklin, Gen. William B., vice-president of Colt's, 32, 73; diary, 144
Frontier Six Shooter, 81; recoil measured, 55; introduced, 84, 100, 125; see also Army Model of 1873

Garrett, Sheriff Pat, quoted, 171
German Government cartridge, 106, 168
Godfrey, Charles J., of New York, firearms dealer, 116
Godfrey, Capt. Edward S., 7th Cavalry, 34, 161, 163
Golcher Bros., of San Francisco, firearms dealer, 118
Gonzales & Schaper, of Galveston, firearms dealer, 118
Gould, A. C., on preference of frontiersmen, 53
Grant, Pres. Ulysses S., 139, 154
Greer, Lieut. John E., of Ordnance Dept., 43, 61, 69; quoted, 58
Grubb, Jos. C., & Co. of Philadelphia, 5, 113, 115

Hains, Wiley G., of Hominy, I. T., 95
Hall, Capt. William Preble, 5th Cavalry, quoted, 77
Handles, 89, 91, 94, 98, 102, 104
Harbison, Hugh, treasurer at Colt's, 153
Harper & Reynolds, of Los Angeles, firearms dealer, 118
Harrington, Gilbert H., patentee, 129
Hart, William S., his pistols, 93, 120
Hegewald, Lieut. John Frederick Charles, 15th Infantry, 91
Henry repeating rifle, 14, 24
Hibbard Spencer & Co., of Chicago, firearms dealer, 115
Hickok, Wild Bill, 97
Hollywood, 88, 119, 120
Honeyman Hardware Co., of Portland, Oregon, 118
Hopkins & Allen, of Norwich, firearms manufacturer, 71

Houston, William R., of Texas, 91
Hulbert, William A., patentee, 71
Hummel, Charles, & Son, of San Antonio, firearms dealer, 115

Imitations, foreign, 133-135, 169
Indians, 13, 14, 24, 26, 34, 135, 139, 160, 162, 170

Janney-Semple Hill & Co., of Minneapolis, firearms dealer, 116
Judson, Edward Zane Caroll, "Ned Buntline," 167

Kelton, Col. John C., invents safety stop, 75
Ketelson & Degetau, of Juarez, firearms dealer, 118
Kipp, Juan H., of Guadalajara, firearms dealer, 118
Kitchener, Major H. E. C., 166
Kittredge, B. & Co., of Cincinnati, firearms dealer, 5, 23, 34, 84, 96, 97, 115, 116; advertisements, 35, 74; end papers
Klondike Rush, 88, 118, 171
Krakauer, Zork & Moye, of Durango, firearms dealer, 118

Langstroth & Co., of Monterey, firearms dealer, 118
Leader, O. W., of Scipio, Okla., 95
Lee, Gen. Fitzhugh, favors Colt for cavalry, 159, 170
Lee, Gen. Robert E., his pistol, 4
Lee, Gen. Stephen D., opinion cited, 170
Le Mat revolver, 8
Le Valley, Salem G., Co. of Buffalo, N. Y., firearms dealer, 118
Lewistown, Mont., 99
Lillie, Gordon W., 99
Little Big Horn, 14, 24
London Agency, 102, 104, 116, 123, 125, 130, 142, 151, 158
London Exhibition of 1851, 137
Lone Ranger, 88
Lovell, J. P., Arms Co., of Boston, 116
Lower, John P., of Denver, firearms dealer, 115

McCall, Jack, 98
McClintock, Maj. W., Supt. at Enfield, quoted, 55

McClung, C. M., & Co., of Knoxville, firearms dealer, 118
McGunnegle, Lieut. George Kennedy, 15th Infantry, 91
McKee, Capt. George W., of Ordnance Dept., 43, 69
McIntosh Hardware Co., of Albuquerque, 118
Marshall Wells Hardware Co., of Duluth, Winnipeg, Spokane and Portland, 116
Mason, William, patentee, 128, 131, 132
Masterson, Bat, 91, 96; letter, 92
Meacham, E. C., Arms Co., of St. Louis, 115
Merritt, Gen. Wesley, 97, 170
Merwin & Bray, of New York, 71
Merwin Hulbert & Co., of New York, firearms dealer, 71; multiball cartridge, 61; revolver, 67; diagrams, 68; dimensions and weights, 69; tested against Colt, 70; advertised, 72
Metallic cartridges, 3, 14, 26, 46, 137, 156; issuance by Ordnance Dept., 17, 62
Metcalfe, Lieut. Henry, of Ordnance Dept., 28
Mexican Border, 88, 118
Mexican Government, 95
Mexican National R.R., 95
Mexican War, 52, 136
Meyer & Geiger, of New York, firearms dealer, 115
Michaelis, Capt. Otho Ernest, ordnance officer in Dept. of Dakota, quoted, 33, 73
Miles, Gen. Nelson A., 58, 91
Miller Bros., of Marsland, Okla., 120
Miller, Morse & Co., of Winnipeg, Manitoba, firearms dealer, 118
Miniatures, see Replicas
Mitchell, Lieut. David Dawson, 15th Infantry, 91
Missoula Mercantile Co., of Montana, 118
Mix, Tom, 120
Model "P," highest serial, 85; serial range, 86; production declines, 119; patents, 128, 131; see also Army Model of 1873
Montgomery Ward & Co., 116
Moore, Daniel, patentee, 71
Moore's, J. P., Sons, of New York, firearms dealer, 115; advertisement, 125

Morgan, Gen. John H., of Kentucky, his pistols, 6
Morrison, Lieut. C. C., of Ordnance Dept., 59
Mosby, Col. John S., used Colt revolver, 160
Multiball cartridge, suggested, 50; experiments, 56, 57; enthusiasm for, 58, 62; tested, 61

National Arms Co., revolver, 15
Navy Model of 1851, 4, 5, 111; converted, 76
Navy Model of 1861, 9, 111
New York Agency, 116
Nez Perces Indians, 34

Olmsted, Frederick L., quoted, 136, 169; 101 Ranch, 120
Open-top Model of 1872, see Army Model of 1872
Orbea Hermanos, of Eibar, 134
Ordnance boards, reports quoted, 15, 28, 30, 31, 39, 44, 59, 61, 66, 70, 71, 76, 79
Ordnance, Chief of (Army), annual reports quoted, 17, 22, 32, 57, 78
Ordnance, Chief of Bureau of (Navy), quoted, 76
Ordnance Memoranda, quoted, 44, 152
Ordnance Notes, quoted, 18, 20, 21, 28, 30, 31, 36, 38-41, 69-71
Otis, Col. Elmer, 8th Cavalry, quoted, 76, 78

Pacific Hardware & Steel Co., of San Francisco, 118
Paine, Ira, shoots Colt against Webley, 54
Paris International Exhibition of 1867, 145
Parnham, Jno. W., of Hillsboro, Texas, 95
Parral gold mine, 95
Parts list, 22
Patagonia Mining Co., 95
Patents, British
June   1, 1867 (Poultney), 144, 172
Oct.   22, 1867 (Adams), 130, 168
Dec.   31, 1868 (Von Oppen), 142
United States
Feb.   25, 1836 (Colt), 3
April   3, 1855 (Rollin White), 10, 11

Patents, United States (Cont.)
April   13, 1858 (Rollin White), 143
Oct.   22, 1861 (Allen), 66
July   19, 1864 (Rupertus), 66
Sept.   20, 1864 (Wood), 144, 172
Oct.   3, 1865 (Crispin), 144, 172
April   7, 1866 (Crowell), 144, 172
April   2, 1867 (Drew), 129
Sept.   15, 1868 (Thuer), 142, 158
Dec.   29, 1868 (Adams), 130, 168
Jan.   4, 1870 (Thuer), 142
Feb.   7, 1871 (Harrington), 130
June   27, 1871 (Forehand), 66
June   29, 1871 (Schofield), 21
July   25, 1871 (Richards), 128, 154
Sept.   19, 1871 (Richards), 102, 128
July   2, 1872 (Mason), 102, 128
April   22, 1873 (Schofield), 21
Oct.   28, 1873 (Rupertus), 66
April   21, 1874 (Williams), 72
Dec.   15, 1874 (Moore), 72
Jan.   19, 1875 (Mason), 102, 128
March   6, 1877 (Moore), 71
March   6, 1877 (Hulbert), 71
Dec.   29, 1885 (Kelton), 75, 165
Paterson Colt, 3
Patton, Gen. George S., Jr., 110
Pawnee Bill, 99
Peacemaker, advertised, 23, 91; deriva-
  tion and nicknames, 84; toys marked,
  135; see also Army Model of 1873
Peck, Lieut. F. E., of Ordnance Dept.,
  79
Petmecky, J. C., of Austin, Texas, fire-
  arms dealer, 115
Philadelphia Centennial of 1876, 51, 97
Philippine Insurrection, 82, 91, 140
Pocket Model of 1849, 111
Pombo, Gen. Amaro, of Mexico, his
  pistols, 32
Post, E. J., & Co., of Albuquerque, fire-
  arms dealer, 116
Poultney, Thomas, patentee, 144
Powell & Clement, of Cincinnati, fire-
  arms dealer, 116
Prices, see Sales
Proofmarks, 44, 103

Quintana Hermanos, of Mexico City,
  firearms dealer, 118

Ramsay, Lieut. George D., of Ordnance
  Dept., 30
Rattlesnake Jake, 99

Rea, W. M., Chief of Ft. Worth police,
  95
Read, Wm., & Sons, of Boston, firearms dealer, 115
Rector & Wilhelmy, of Omaha, firearms
  dealer, 118
Reed, Wm., of Antelope Springs, Colo.,
  95
Reilly, Capt. J. W., of Ordnance Dept.,
  suggests multiball, 50
Remington, E., & Sons, 7, 43, 58
Remington, Frederic, 138, 139, 164
Remington Model of 1875, tested against
  Colt and Schofield, 36, 132; dimen-
  sions, weights and firing, 38; endur-
  ance and fouling, 39; rust test, 37;
  diagrams, 40, 42, 43; purchased by
  Egypt, 42, 163; tested in .45 calibre
  at Springfield, 43
Remington percussion revolver, 7, 8;
  conversion of, 10, 11, 12, 15, 16
Remington single shot pistol, 7, 13;
  selected, 15, 16; ammunition, 17
Reno, Major Marcus A., 7th Cavalry,
  24, 162
Replicas, toy, 133, 140; miniature, 135
Revillon Freres, of Edmonton, Alberta,
  118
Richards, Charles B., 18, 128, 154
Richards Conversion, 18, 19; serial
  range, 111; cost, 112; patents, 128, 130,
  154
Richards & Conover, of Kansas City,
  firearms dealer, 116
Rifling, 22, 101, 108
Ripley, Lieut. H. L., 3rd Cavalry,
  quoted, 78
Rimfire .44, Single Action, 100, 127;
  serial numbers, 113
Rivera, Gen. Aureliano, of Mexico, his
  pistols, 114
Rockwell, Lieut. James, Jr., of Ord-
  nance Dept., 36, 64
Rodriguez, Felipe, 95
Rodriguez, Tibucio, 95
Roosevelt, Theodore, on preference of
  ranchmen, 53, 139
Root, Elisha K., 144, 155
Rosser, Gen. Thomas L., favors Colt for
  cavalry, 159
Royal Navy, orders London Colt, 137
Rupertus, Jacob, of Philadelphia,
  patentee, 66

Sabre, uselessness in Indian warfare, 16, 161; eclipsed by revolver, 137
Sales and prices, 7, 12, 13, 35, 37, 74, 98, 113, 115, 119, 151, 156
Sanford, Maj. George B., 1st Cavalry, quoted, 14
San Francisco Agency, 116
San Antonio Police Dept., 95, 119
Salt Lake Hardware Co., 116
Schofield, Maj. George W., 10th Cavalry, submits design, 21, 28, 30, 32; death of, 35
Schofield Gen. John M., Secretary of War, 32
Schofield, Smith & Wesson, 14; tested, 21, 28; approved, 30; purchased, 32; procurements and issues, 33; advertised, 35, 74; tested against Colt and Remington, 36; dimensions, weights and firing, 38; rust test, 38, 47; endurance and fouling, 39; diagrams, 34, 41, 42, 43; stamping, 44; defended, 47, 49; exhibited at Philadelphia, 52; fitted with Kelton safety, 75; criticized, 32, 77
Schuyler, Hartley & Graham, of New York, firearms dealer, 5, 35, 64, 113, 115; advertisement, 98
Schoverling, Daly & Gales, of New York, firearms dealer, 115
Schwabacher & Co., of Seattle, firearms dealer, 118
Seattle Hardware Co., of Portland, Oregon, 118
Serial Numbers, 27, 83, 101-103, 111; table, 86; of Thuer, 157
Simmons Hardware Co., of St. Louis, 115; letter, 116
Single Action Army, 84, 117; see also Army Model of 1873
Sioux Indians, 13, 14, 24, 26, 139
Shapleigh Hardware Co., of St. Louis, 118
Sharps Rifle, 14, 24, 139, 169
Sheridan, Gen. Philip H., his pistols, 8, 9; comment on pistols, 50
Sherman, Gen. William Tecumseh, 16; comment on Colt revolver, 49
Smith, Chas., of Silver City, N. M., 95
Smith & Wesson, 10, 144, 146; American model, 14, 15, 17, 31, 49; tested against Colt, 20; Model of 1873, 21; Russian Model, 28, 29, 35; double action .38; tested against Colt, 78-80

Smith, Lieut. William H., 10th Cavalry, quoted, 165
Smokeless powder, 101
Smoot, W. S., superintendent at Remington's, pistols, 43
Snake Creek, 34
Soo Ho Sam, 95
Spanish-American War, 140
Special Target Model, 104, 108, 124
Speer Hardware Co., of Ft. Smith, Arkansas, 118
Spencer repeating rifle, 24, 161, 170
Springfield Armory, 22, 26, 28, 36, 42, 47, 57, 64, 80, 135, 168
Springfield rifle, 14, 24, 50, 56, 161
Stafford, Lieut. Stephen Randall, 15th Infantry, 91
Stauffer, Eshleman & Co., of New Orleans, firearms dealer, 118
Steinfeld, A., & Co., of Tucson, firearms dealer, 118
Stuart, Granville, cattleman, 98
Swaine, Lt. Col. Peter Tyler, 15th Infantry, 90
Swift, Lieut. Eben, 5th Cavalry, quoted, 62

Territorial Prison, Yuma, 95
Texas Rangers, 136
Texas, revolvers in, 137, 140, 169
Thuer Conversion, 12, 141, 144, 147; tested by War Office, 148; tested at Woolwich, 150; submitted to U. S. Ordnance Dept., 152; calibres, 155; loading directions, 156; price, 151, 156
Thuer, F. Alexander, inventor, 141, 154
Tiger Gold Co., 95
Tips, Walter, of Austin, Texas, firearms dealer, 116
Tisdall, Charles E., of Vancouver, firearms dealer, 118
Tomboy gold mine, at Telluride, 95
Trademark, 103
Tranter revolver, 137
Tryon, E. K., Jr., & Co., of Philadelphia firearms dealer, 115

Umbeyla Pass, 82
Union Army, percussion Colt in, 5, 7
Union Metallic Cartridge Co., 10, 100
U. S. Mounted Rifles, 136
U. S. Supreme Court, 139, 172

Variations, rimfire, 100, 129; with long
  handle, 104; with D. A. cylinder, 105,
  109
Vidmer, Capt. George, 11th Cavalry,
  quoted, 170
Von Lengerke & Antoine, of Chicago,
  firearms dealer, 118
Von Oppen, Baron Frederic A. K. W.,
  agent at London, 142, 163; quoted,
  55, 147

Wadsworth, Henry C., of Worcester,
  firearms manufacturer, 66
Wagon Box fight, 15
Walker, Capt. Samuel H., 5, 84, 136
Wallace, Lieut. George G., 7th Cavalry,
  quoted, 24, 162
Walsh, John Henry, reports Colt-Web-
  ley trial, 55
Waters, Lieut. Basil Norris, 15th In-
  fantry, 91
Webb, Walter Prescott, quoted, fore-
  word, 136
Webley, H., shoots his pistol against
  Colt, 55
Webley revolver, 54; recoil measured, 55
Weir, Harry, Sec'y for Cowboy's Race,
  95
Weldrun, Robt. D., of Telluride, 95
Wells-Fargo & Co., 95
Werndl rifle and revolver, 50
Wesson, Daniel B., 32, 130

Wexell & Degress, of New York and
  Mexico City, firearms dealer, 115
White, Rollin, his patent, 10, 128, 129,
  139, 141, 143, 144, 146, 154
Whitney revolver, 15
Whitneyville Colt, 5
Willmanns, F., & Co., of Durango, fire-
  arms dealer, 118
Wilson, Gen. James H., quoted, 170
Windolph, Sgt. Charles A., 7th Cavalry,
  24, 162
Winchester, Oliver F., 132
Winchester Repeating Arms Co., 115,
  120, 132
Winchester rifle, 81, 84, 99, 100, 121,
  125, 132, 134, 139, 171
Wister, Owen, The Virginian, 88
Wood, Stephen W., patentee, 144
Wood, Valance & Co., of Hamilton,
  Ontario, firearms dealer, 118
Woolwich Arsenal, 150
World War I, 88, 119
World War II, 85
Wright, Capt. E. M., of Ordnance Dept.,
  56, 57, 59
Wyoming Stock Growers Ass'n, 171

XIT Ranch, 140

Yellowstone Expedition of 1873, 162

Zeckendorf, L., & Co., of Tucson, firearms dealer, 118